D1267726

Everyone's
Kids'
Books

DISCARDED BY HUNTER LIBRARY WCU

DISCARDED BY HUNTER LIBRARY WCU

Copyright © 2000 by Everyone's Books
Cover photography © 2000 by Julie Simms
Book design by Julie Simms
Printed and bound in the United States

All rights reserved.
No part of this book may be reproduced
in any form or by any means
without permission from the publisher:
Everyone's Books, 23 Elliot Street,
Brattleboro, Vermont 05301   802-254-8160

ISBN: 09703816-0-3

Everyone's Kids' Books

A Guide to Multicultural, Socially Conscious Books for Children

Nancy Braus
Molly Geidel

Everyone's Books

Brattleboro, Vermont

Contents

Introduction   vi

Acknowledgements   xi

African-American History
and Current Affairs   1

African-American Picture Books
and Literature   6

Caribbean Region   35

African Heritage and Life   37

Latin-American Heritage   48

Books in Spanish and Bilingual Books   59

Native-American Heritage   66

Asian Heritage   82

European and Russian Heritage   98

Jewish-American and Holocaust Literature   100

The Middle East   104

Our Multicultural Society   106

Adoption   112

Family Diversity   117

HUNTER LIBRARY
WESTERN CAROLINA UNIVERSITY

People Around the World   120

Gay and Lesbian Books   127

War and Peace, Justice and Righteous Acts   131

Dealing with Violence and Injustice   141

Strong Girls and Women:
Picture Books and Literature   146

Strong Girls and Women:
History and Current Issues   159

Changing Boys: Challenging Stereotypes   168

Science and Nature   172

Books for Parents and Teachers   178

Index by Title and Author   188

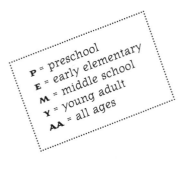

P = preschool
E = early elementary
M = middle school
Y = young adult
AA = all ages

HUNTL R LIBRARY
WESTERN CAROLINA UNIVERSIT

Introduction

Fifteen years ago, when we opened Everyone's Books, a progressive, independent bookstore, one of the main goals was to create a high-quality, comprehensive, multicultural children's section, including books about strong girls and women, nature and other areas of special interest. Because the store was located in a small town, a catalog seemed like a great way to enable the children's books to find a wide audience. The original annotated list of the books I found most significant has grown over the years, and has outgrown the format of a catalog.

This book is an attempt to collect the most exciting, important, in-print books for children about a broad range of cultures, family issues and subjects of interest to parents, teachers and others wanting to help broaden and humanize children's experiences through reading. Also included are some adult books about parenting and teaching for peace, social justice and understanding diversity.

In many ways, reading has become less important for many young people, edged out by the many forms of electronic media available to them. However, the availability of high-quality, exciting and even radical children's books makes the reading experience more valuable now than ever before. The lack of creativity, originality and progressive values in television, CD-Roms and other media aimed at kids is appalling, and commercialism is thoroughly pervasive in most mass media. Reading and discussing remains an important way, maybe the best way, to help kids become critical thinkers and lifelong learners.

I read many of the older books to my now nearly grown daughters when they were younger. Now my 20-year-old daughter, Molly, is reading and reviewing many of the newest books, and we are collaborating on this book. Feedback on these books comes from teachers, parents, librarians and children who are customers and friends. I am lucky to have so many intelligent, well-read and thoughtful people to help with reading and thinking about kids' books.

The term *multicultural* has an unexpected and special meaning in my family—in addition to my two older birth-daughters, we adopted Laura from Colombia seven years ago, and learned later that she is deaf. We have become a family that must navigate the social and linguistic worlds of deaf and hearing cultures daily. This has opened our eyes and minds in ways we never imagined, and helped us understand, far better than ever before, the world of the "other" in this American life. While many people accept Laura easily and naturally, we are often faced with both children and adults who cannot seem to see past her deafness to interact with our wonderful child.

Thanks to the many people over the years who have given us their opinions and criticism of books and previous catalogs. Thank you also to the many customers who have assured us that what we are doing is necessary and unique, and that a huge super-store does not carry that special book on adoption, or Korea, or gay teens, or Oaxaca, or labor, or growing up biracial or...

We welcome visitors to our Southern Vermont store and are always happy to discuss children's books, or fill orders in person, on the telephone, or at our e-mail address. Contact us at:

Everyone's Books
23 Elliot Street
Brattleboro, Vermont 05301
(802) 254-8160
e-mail: solarhom@sover.net

The information on prices won't be valid for long; it will probably be invalid even as this book becomes available. However, this information does give a close approximation of what you can expect to pay for a given book. Many of the low-cost paperback books are also available in hardcover and/or library binding. The price listed here is the lowest cost for the book in the early part of the year 2000.

The descriptions of the books include age guidelines; these are only suggestions, as you know the children who will be reading these books. P = Preschool, E = Early elementary, M = Middle grades, Y = Young adult, AA = All ages

The bibliographic data is easy to obtain at this point—from any bookstore, library or on line. Here we present many years' worth of opinions and information that may be a bit harder to obtain. In an effort to keep the book readable and the cost low, we decided not to list publication information.

We have attempted to place books in categories where we feel a person would be most likely to expect to find them. That said, almost all of the best books fit into two, three or more categories.

The lists on the opposite page are strictly personal preference; these are books that we love and have read many times.

Nancy Braus

Our Favorite Books

Picture books:

All the Colors We Are, 108
Children Just Like Me, 122
The First Strawberries, 68
I Look Like a Girl, 149
Molly Bannaky, 152
A Mother for Choco, 113
Nine O'Clock Lullaby, 125
Oliver Button Is a Sissy, 169
On the Day You Were Born, 173
The Paper Bag Princess, 153
The Red Comb, 64
Soul Looks Back in Wonder, 11
Under the Lemon Moon, 52
Wilma Unlimited, 19

Novels and short-story collections:

Bud, Not Buddy, 11
Dragonwings, 97
*Fearless Girls, Wise Women and Brave Sisters:
   Heroines and Folktales from Around the World*, 154
A Girl Named Disaster, 39
Roll of Thunder, Hear My Cry, 30
Shabanu, Daughter of the Wind, 155
The Watsons Go to Birmingham—1963, 10

History/Non-fiction for older kids:

The Autobiography of Malcolm X, 5
*Deal With It! A Whole New Approach to Your Body, Brain
   and Life as a Gurl*, 161
A Drawing in the Sand: The Story of African-American Art, 8
Hear These Voices: Youth at the Edge of the Millennium, 141
People's History of the United States, 187
Real Girl, Real World: Tools for Finding Your True Self, 162
*The Shared Heart: Portraits and Stories Celebrating Lesbian, Gay and
   Bisexual Young People*, 129

Acknowledgements

A special thank you to the following people for their time and energy in this project:

Jane Braus, our mother and grandmother, for a thorough and thoughtful proofreading job.

Julie Simms, for moving this project from printed pages to an actual book. Julie's presence kept us on task and moving ahead. She also inspired us with her design ideas and skills.

Pam Fuller, for editing this when we were naïve enough to think it was ready for publication!

Rosita, for additional proofreading and her expertise in Spanish.

Alicia Jacobsen, for her eagerness to discuss children's books at length, both in person and currently by e-mail from her home in West Africa.

Karen Saunders, for her educated and constructive reading of this work before publication.

The extended and immediate family, Jane and Jay Braus, Pat, Paul, Peter and Kaija Braus, Rich Geidel, Janie and Laura, and Ed Lopez, Dan and Jay, all of whom love reading and helped us become people who can appreciate good books.

Thank you to the wonderful children who are seen bouncing on the book's cover: Mira, Willow, Joy, Amy, Miya, Noah and Laura.

And thank you to the special and dedicated authors of children's books who are writing with a peaceful, equitable and truly multicultural vision.

P = preschool
E = early elementary
M = middle school
Y = young adult
AA = all ages

African-American History and Current Affairs

A Weed Is a Flower
Aliki
This is a fascinating look at the famous scientist George Washington Carver. Carver was a multi-talented man whose work in plant biology was a great help to southern sharecroppers. $5.95 **E**

The Underground Railroad E 450 .B53 1995
Raymond Bial
This thematically organized description of the Underground Railroad includes photos of slave quarters, secret passages and notices offering rewards for the capture of runaways. In an accessible, easy-to-read style, the book shows us how an impressive network was created by many courageous slaves and their allies. $5.95 **P, E**

Through My Eyes F 379 .N59 N435 1999
Ruby Bridges
In the fall of 1960, Ruby Bridges was chosen to be the first and only black child to attend her elementary school in Baton Rouge. She had to be marched through hundreds of protesters and went to first grade alone, since for most of the year all the white parents pulled their children out of school. Amazing photographs show an adorable, brave and sometimes worried little girl in stark contrast to the hateful protesters she faced outside her school every day. The story includes good background information about the Civil Rights Movement. $16.95 **E**

The National Civil Rights Museum Celebrates Everyday People

Alice Faye Duncan

This book is filled with photographs and text about the National Civil Rights Museum in the former Lorraine Motel in Memphis, Tennessee, location of Dr. Martin Luther King, Jr.'s assassination. The museum opened in 1991 as a celebration of the lives of the many people who played a role in the Civil Rights Movement of the 1950s and '60s. Photos in the book include some of children of different races visiting the museum. $6.95 **E**

I Was Born a Slave: The Story of Harriet Jacobs

Jennifer Fleischner   E 450 . F54 1997

This is an adaptation for young people of the book *Incidents in the Life of a Slave Girl*, by Harriet Jacobs, a famous and still-read book published in 1861. The life Jacobs was forced to lead as a slave and her harrowing, long ordeal escaping from slavery again reveal the depth of the depravity of the slave system. Harriet Jacobs possessed incredible strength, intelligence and spirit, to survive, write her life story and continue to work for others throughout her life. $12.95 **M**

Bound for America: The Forced Migration of Africans to the New World

James Haskins and Kathleen Benson

This book is for kids who know something about slavery but want to understand more about its origins, about why and how Europeans could have kidnapped thousands and thousands of people and created a system of slavery different than anything ever seen in human history. The book, organized thematically, gives historical background about slavery and what else was going on in Europe and Africa when the kidnapping started. Maps, photographs, old drawings and Floyd Cooper's incredible paintings depict the conditions slaves endured on the voyage to America. $18.00 **E**

Book of Black Heroes from A to Z
Wade Hudson

From Ira Aldrich, an actor who had to emigrate to Europe to get jobs, through sculptor Edmonia Lewis, to Shaka Zulu, the Southern African warrior, the 50 famous and should-be-famous heroes portrayed in this book all have interesting, inspiring stories. Most stories are accompanied by photos. $7.95 **E, M**

Book of Black Heroes Volume II: Great Women in the Struggle
Toyomi Igus

While many of the women whose photos and stories appear in this book are famous internationally, such as Coretta Scott King and Miriam Makeba, others are virtually unknown. All are women of amazing accomplishments, whether personal or in the public service arena. $10.95 **M, Y**

Our America: Life and Death on the South Side of Chicago
LeAlan Jones and Lloyd Newman

Many listeners of National Public Radio one day heard the voices of two young men probing the death of five-year-old Eric Morse, dropped by ten- and eleven-year-old boys from the window of a high-rise in an inner-city project. These same clear-eyed, intelligent boys, with producer David Isay, now tell their stories in a book, with photographs, of life in the other America. For anyone interested in the real-life stories of the poorest black Americans, told with dignity and compassion from the inside, this is the book. $14.00 **Y**

This Strange New Feeling
Julius Lester

Lester retold the three love stories in this book from historical documents of the time. Each couple falls in love and obtains their freedom from slavery through bravery, hardship, cleverness and a good dose of luck. The dramatic tales help us understand what it may have felt to savor the first moments of freedom. $4.50 **Y**

Long Journey Home
Julius Lester   PZ 7, L5629 Lo3
Six true tales of "common folk" from black history, newly retold.
Moving and readable. $4.50   Y

Escape From Slavery: The Boyhood of Frederick Douglass in His Own Words
Edited and illustrated by Michael McCurdy
In this beautiful volume, McCurdy has excerpted sections from the
first of Frederick Douglass's autobiographies. The portions contained in this book are exciting, horrifying and very readable. The
woodcut illustrations add a new dimension to this classic narrative.
$6.99   M

Black Americans: A History in Their Own Words
Milton Meltzer
Documents including speeches, letters and memoirs, tracing black
history from slavery to freedom through the early 1980s. $9.95   AA

Frederick Douglass: The Last Day of Slavery
William Miller
Miller conveys Frederick Douglass's thoughts and feelings during
his formative years as a plantation slave. A powerful introduction to
the tragedy of slavery. $5.95   P, E

Black and Red: Portraits of Independent Spirits
Morgan Monceaux and Ruth Katcher
Black Americans and Native Americans both played a major role in
the Old West. Monceaux's memorable multi-media artwork and
words convey some of the variety of famous and little-known figures who were cowboys, nurses, entrepreneurs, brave tribal chiefs,
stagecoach drivers and more. The West represented freedom for
many blacks, leaving the racial barriers of the more established
states, but for Native Americans, the West was truly the last fron-
tier. Many times, the two came together to aid one another and
even live together. $18.00   M   E 185, 97, 073 H67   WCU Gen

Coming of Age in Mississippi
Anne Moody

Anne Moody grew up just before the Civil Rights years; in this classic memoir she recounts her experiences both before and at the beginning of the movement. This version has been expanded. $6.99 Y

E185.97. M65 A3

Jackie Robinson and the Story of All-Black Baseball
Jim O'Connor

This book focuses on the Negro Leagues, illustrating a piece of sports history many kids know little about. The legacy of discrimination in the U.S., and the descriptions of many talented black players in early baseball, make for absorbing reading. $2.95 E

The Year They Walked
Beatrice Seigel

A fascinating account of that extraordinary year, 1956, when black people in Montgomery, Alabama, got together to express their rage about segregation, thus beginning the long struggle for its end. $15.00 M

Follow in Their Footsteps: Biographies of Ten Outstanding African Americans
Glenette Tilley Turner

This book includes biographies of Thurgood Marshall, Carter G. Woodson, Bessie Coleman, Malcolm X and Alex Haley, as well as stories of lesser-known people like sculptor Edmonia Lewis and entrepreneur A. G. Gaston. The biographies are fun to read, and after each story the author has written a play about the subject's life for kids to act out. $7.99 E, M

The Autobiography of Malcolm X
This is certainly not a new book, but it is definitely one of the most influential ones written in the last 30 years. It has had a profound impact on the lives of generations of teenagers and is great for provoking discussion about race, religion, politics and personal transformation. $6.99 Y

E185.97.L5 A3

P = preschool

E = early elementary

M = middle school

Y = young adult

AA = all ages

African–American Picture Books and Literature

In for Winter, Out for Spring
Arnold Adoff

"I like my real name short and my hair real long/ I am the youngest and I belong," is how the narrator of this story proudly introduces herself. She goes on to explain about the weather, bugs, mice and other aspects of life in the country. Poetry by Adoff and illustrations by Jerry Pinkney are a winning combination in this book about childhood, family life and outdoor play around the seasons. $7.00 **P, E**

Brothers of the Night
Debbie Allen

This is a very cool adaptation of the story "The Twelve Dancing Princesses." Reverend Knight has a problem. Every morning, his twelve sons' shoes are worn to shreads, even though the boys claim to be asleep in their one, large bed all night. After many house-keepers, the Reverend finally hires Sunday, a wise and slightly magical woman who follows the boys at night and discovers their secret life of dancing away the night! A funny, warm, family story that takes place in "a little village called Harlem." The illustrations by Kadir Nelson are funny and appealing. $15.99 **P,E**

Steal Away
Jennifer Armstrong

Susannah and Bethlehem are runaways from southern slavery. Susannah is a Vermont girl who becomes orphaned and is sent to live on her uncle's plantation. She is "given" Bethlehem as her slave. Once they decide to leave the South and the system of slavery, the girls must travel the long and dangerous route from Virginia to Vermont on foot, but they succeed together and become friends for life. $4.95 **M** P27. A73367 st

No Mirrors in My Nana's House

Ysaye M. Barnwell

"There were no mirrors in my nana's house/no mirrors in my nana's house/so the beauty I saw in everything/the beauty in everything/ was in her eyes/like the rising of the sun." So begins this wonderful song written by Ysaye M. Barnwell and sung by her a cappela group, Sweet Honey in the Rock. Synthia Saint James's beautiful paintings perfectly complement the words to the song, creating a celebration of self-confidence and inner beauty. A CD of Sweet Honey singing the song is included. $18.00 **E**

Forever Friends

Candy Dawson Boyd

Twelve-year-old Toni is facing a challenging entrance exam for the secondary school her parents want her to attend. When one of her best friends is killed in an accident, Toni's grief is intense. With the help of her family and community she comes to terms with the death. $4.99 **M, Y**

Wagon Wheels

Barbara Brenner

Wagon Wheels is an easy-to-read, exciting and true story of a black pioneer family, a father and three sons, who travel from Kentucky to a homestead in Kansas. A good eye-opener about the black West and about Native-American history. $3.75 **P, E**

PZ7.B7518 Wag

Imani's Gift at Kwanzaa

Denise Burden-Patman

Imani's grandmother shows her a little bit about Kwanzaa, especially the principle of Umoja, or unity, when she encourages Imani to welcome a girl into her family who has had a difficult life. Imani's enjoyment of Kwanzaa is coupled with an explanation of its basic ideas and celebrations. $4.95 **P, E**

PZ7.B91615 Im

A Drawing in the Sand: The Story of African-American Art

Jerry Butler

Jerry Butler's work is to be savored, read and looked at again and again. In the unique style of his own collage and works in various media, reproductions of some of the finest work of other artists and his stunning graphic design, Butler tells his own story as well as those of many talented African-American artists. The author began his art "career" as a child drawing in the red dirt outside his Mississippi farmhouse, encouraged by his wise and respected grandmother, and we hope he will be creating for many years to come. $24.95 **AA**

Stories Julian Tells

Ann Cameron

Imaginative Julian, his brother Huey and their parents' day-to-day lives will be sure to make you smile. The book is narrated by Julian and is set up as a series of short stories, including "Catalog Cats," "Pudding Like a Night on the Sea" and "Gloria Who Might be my Best Friend." $4.99 **E** PZ7. C1427 St

More Stories Julian Tells

Ann Cameron

Julian's back, and this time his best friend Gloria is there to add even more humor and excitement to his and Huey's adventures. Includes the classic "A Day When Frogs Wear Shoes." $4.99 **E**

PZ7. C1427 Mo

Julian's Glorious Summer

Ann Cameron

Julian's fear of bicycle riding and his penchant for storytelling get him into trouble with both his father and Gloria. $3.99 **E**

Stories Huey Tells
Ann Cameron
Finally, Huey gets to tell some stories of his own! His voice, though different than his brother Julian's, is just as much fun to hear, and his stories, about cooking, animal tracking and Africa, among other things, are always entertaining. $4.99 E

To Be a Drum
Evelyn Coleman
The father of two young children tells them the story of black history, using drums as the string that links the past and present, and drums that link the earth and the people. The illustrations are original and lively mixed-media paintings. $16.95 E

White Socks Only
Evelyn Coleman
A spirited young girl decides she's going to town to see if it's really hot enough to fry an egg on the sidewalk. She sneaks into town dressed in her Sunday best and fries the egg, then goes to quench her thirst at a drinking fountain. Seeing a "whites only" sign, she takes off her shoes and steps up to the fountain in her bright white socks. When a white man tries to stop her, the local black community comes together to support her. $6.95 E

So Much
Trish Cooke
This large picture book for very young children begins with Mom and baby at home. A string of relatives arrives, each with his or her own way of hugging, squeezing, kissing and loving the baby. When Daddy finally arrives home, to a packed and happy home, it is the baby he hugs first. Helen Oxenbury's illustrations help create the warmth and exuberance of this extended African-American family. $6.99 P   PZ7.C77 494 So

Coming Home: From the Life of Langston Hughes
Floyd Cooper

Out of a childhood spent largely alone and in poverty, as a single child in a rural home with his grandmother, emerged one of the great poetic voices of this century. This picture book introduces children to Langston Hughes, a visionary and influential figure, in an easily accessible picture book. $5.99 **AA**

Sweet Words So Brave: The Story of African-American Literature
Barbara Curry and James Michael Brody

The lives and works of authors, from those early slaves who told the still retold trickster tales, to current writers such as Maya Angelou and Alice Walker, are presented here. The illustrator Jerry Butler's book design and paintings will take your breath away: they are outstanding. The book manages to weave the lives of the authors into a visual and literary panorama of history, presented in a way that is difficult to resist. $24.95 **M, Y**

The Watsons Go to Birmingham—1963
Christopher Paul Curtis

This first novel has received rave reviews for both its memorable narrator and its accurate rendering of black life in 1963. Fourth-grader Kenny Watson and his family live in Flint, Michigan; Kenny describes his family life in hilarious detail. When they decide to pay a visit to relatives in the South, the Watsons witness the violence and Jim Crow-era discrimination of the Old South as well as the beginning of the massive changes occurring there. $4.99 **E, M**

Bud, Not Buddy
Christopher Paul Curtis

This second novel by the talented author of
The Watsons Go to Birmingham—1963 was
awarded the Newbery (first to a black male
author) AND the Coretta Scott King award.
Bud is an orphan in Flint, Michigan, during
the Great Depression, whose beloved mother has been dead for the past four of his
ten years. When he is sent to an abusive
foster home, he leaves and sets out to follow the clues to his identity left behind
by his mother. In his search, he stumbles onto the jazz music scene and becomes
part of the musical family comprised of "Herman E.
Calloway and the Dusky Devastators of the Depression." Through
all his adventures, Bud is feisty, personable and a great window
onto black life in 1936. Two of the main characters are drawn from
the author's own grandfathers! $15.95 **M**

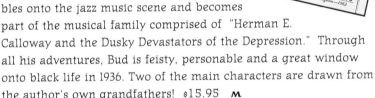

PZ7.C94137 B4

Soul Looks Back in Wonder
Illustrated by Tom Feelings

This book is a true wonder. The winner of a Coretta Scott King
Award, it contains some of the most stunning artwork in any picture book. Tom Feelings created the thirteen pieces of art and then
approached various literary figures, including Maya Angelou and
Lucille Clifton, who wrote poems to go with the artwork. The poems
and the art can be appreciat-
ed on many levels and will
appeal to all ages of children
and adults. $6.99 **AA**

PS591.N4 S58

Dust from Old Bones
Sandra Forrester

In an engaging story for middle-grade readers, Sandra Forrester shows us the unique world of the 19th-century Louisiana Creoles, people of mixed race who lived in New Orleans as second-class citizens. At first, Simone is jealous of her cousin Claire-Marie, who looks almost white and soon will be able to attend debutante balls and find a white man to be her "protector." But Simone begins to see that Claire-Marie's life is not as wonderful as it seems and that there is more to life than debutante balls. She begins to see the injustice of slavery as well as of her own plight as a girl somewhere between slavery and freedom. $16.00 **M**

Grandmama's Joy
Eloise Greenfield

Rhondy and her grandmother usually know just what to do to cheer each other up. But this time, Grandma's sad look won't go away, even when Rhondy dresses up in dangly earrings and sings her a song or finds a perfect rock from the garden. Finally Grandma tells Rhondy she is sad because she has to sell the house they have lived in together for so long. Rhondy knows she needs to think of something extra special to make grandmama smile again; she finally decides to help tell the story of how they came to live together, how she came to be her grandmother's joy. This is a lovely, moving story, with drawings by Carole Byard. $5.99 **P, E**

Night on Neighborhood Street
Eloise Greenfield

Beautiful paintings by Jan Spivey Gilchrist enhance Greenfield's poems about friends, neighbors, kids, music and the joys of sharing the evening with neighbors. $5.99 **P, E**

PS3557, R37416 N5

The Last Safe House: A Story of the Underground Railroad

Barbara Greenwood

This book is presented in a unique format: the fictional stories of Johanna, a 12-year-old white girl from Canada, and Eliza, a runaway slave, are interspersed with maps, facts about the Underground Railroad, project and activity ideas, recipes and more. Heather Collins contributes diagrams, maps and lively drawings of Johanna and Eliza. $9.95 **E, M**

Mary Had a Little Lamb

Sarah Josepha Hale/photographs by Bruce MacMillan

Wonderful illustrations of a contemporary Mary, a black child with glasses and yellow overalls and her well-cared-for lamb, bring a completely new flavor to an old rhyme. The photographer includes information about his choice of "Mary," and other information children and adults will be fascinated to learn. $4.99 **P**

P28.3 .H188 M3

Books by

Virginia Hamilton Virginia Hamilton is one of the best-known and best-loved names in the children's book world. Her works are time-and-again original.

Her Stories: Folktales, Fairy Tales and True Tales

It is a treat to behold this award-winning book of stories told by generations of African-American women. Many are fantasy, but the three personal accounts (true tales) are facinating as well. The illustrators, Leo and Diane Dillon, have outdone themselves, helping to create a masterpiece that can be enjoyed by people of all ages. $19.95 **AA**

GR111 .447 H35

When Birds Could Talk and Bats Could Sing

In this work, Hamilton retells stories of birds, bats and other creatures of the natural world acting suspiciously like their human neighbors. These stories are from slavery times and are beautifully illustrated by Barry Moser. $17.95 **E, M**

Sweet Whispers, Brother Rush

Powerful family story of loss and finding love after a crisis. Both an intriguing ghost story and a realistic portrait of a teenage girl.
$4.99   Y   PZ7 . H 1826 SW

The People Could Fly

Wonderful collection of African-American folktales retold by the author and illustrated by Leo and Diane Dillon. Great for all ages, including adults. $13.00, $21.95 (HARDCOVER BOOK AND AUDIOTAPE), $9.95 (AUDIOTAPE) AA

Many Thousand Gone: African Americans from Slavery to Freedom

Virginia Hamilton retells the story of slavery, from the earliest kidnappings of young Africans through emancipation. The stories tell of the lives of many different slaves remembered for their bravery, intelligence and, in some cases, their tragic fates. They are all fascinating and should engage the most reluctant reader of history.
$12.00 M

xxxx

The Gift Giver

Joyce Hansen

Doris and her friends think Amir is strange when he moves to their Bronx neighborhood at the end of fifth grade. He doesn't play basketball, just sits and watches and thinks all the time, and he never teases other kids the way everyone else does. But Amir always knows how to help Doris and the rest of her friends on 163rd street through problems with family, school and other kids. He and Doris become best friends, but he is a foster child and must move again the next fall. The story is beautifully written, and Doris is a wonderful character who grows up a lot in the short summer she spends with Amir. $6.95 E, M

Which Way Freedom?

Joyce Hansen

One of Obi's earliest memories is the agony of being sold away from his mother. He is determined to locate her again, so when the upheaval of the Civil War makes an escape possible, Obi and his friend Easter take advantage of the situation. They have many dangerous, sometimes exciting adventures, and eventually Obi joins a black regiment in the Union Army. A fascinating view of little-known history of the Civil War by a terrific writer. $4.95 **M**

Out from This Place

Joyce Hansen

Easter, Obi's friend in *Which Way Freedom*, experiences the Civil War very differently than Obi does; this book is her story. After escaping from slavery, she is determined to return for Jason, a boy she has cared for since he was a baby. She bravely returns to the plantation, escapes again and then must search for Obi before she can truly begin her life as a free woman. $4.50 **M**

The Heart Calls Home

Joyce Hansen

This novel of Reconstruction follows Obi in his search to find Easter after his Union Army work is through, to build a new life. Strong images in this book include the lynchings that began in that period, the many displaced former slave children and the extended family created by those who labored together under slavery. Obi and Easter faced the problems of where to live, how to earn a living and how to help others younger or with even fewer resources, all with great dignity and persistence. $16.95 **M**

I Remember "121"

Francine Haskins

The author shares memories of the 1950s in Washington, D.C., in her extended family home. The personalities in her close-knit African-American neighborhood are humorously and lovingly described. $13.99 **P, E**

Amazing Grace

Mary Hoffman

Grace's favorite activity is acting out all kinds of stories. She is sure she can be Peter Pan in her class play, even when the rest of the kids tell her Peter Pan is neither black nor female. Of course, she makes a memorable Peter Pan. Grace is smart, lively and funny. Adults and children alike will enjoy her story, as well as the illustrations by Caroline Binch. This book has become something of a classic. $15.95 **P, E**

Boundless Grace

Mary Hoffman

Grace feels her family isn't complete, as her father left when she was small and now lives with his new family in Africa. When her father saves up money and sends for her, she and her grandmother make the trip to Gambia. She discovers a new family and a new world. Wonderful, brightly colored illustrations of Grace's trip fill the book. $14.99 **P, E**

Happy to Be Nappy

bell hooks

bell hooks has been published many times before as an author of highly regarded feminist nonfiction, but this is her first children's book. The text, all about the pleasures of "nappy hair," is complemented by Chris Raschka's original, fun illustrations. The exuberant mood of this book will catch children, and they'll want to look through it over and over. $14.99 **P, E**

Freedom's Fruit

William Hooks

Based on a story told to the author as a young boy in North Carolina, this haunting tale of a conjure woman and her daring plan to free her daughter and her beloved from slavery is original and memorable. When Mama Marina hears that her daughter and Nathan are to be separated, she tells them to eat conjured grapes. They will become very ill, but not die. As they lie apparently dying, Mama Marina will take all her money and buy their freedom, as two dying slaves are worthless. $16.00 **E**

B
C **Sweet Clara and the Freedom Quilt**
Deborah Hopkinson
Clara is only 11 years old when she is sold away from her mother. At the new plantation an elderly woman teaches her how to do fine stitching, and she gets a job as a seamstress. Clara remembers the vow she made to return to her mother, and stitches a quilt-map of the Ohio River. She escapes, finds her mother and leaves the quilt behind for others in need. Highly recommended. $6.99 **P, E**

B **Bright Eyes, Brown Skin**
Cheryl Willis Hudson
Simple poetry and bright pictures show four confident, curious, energetic African-American children at day care. $6.95 **P**

B **Pass It On: African-American Poetry for Children**
Selected by Wade Hudson
Here is a collection of poems by Langston Hughes, Gwendolyn Brooks, Countee Cullen and many contemporary poets, with wonderful illustrations by Floyd Cooper. $14.95 **P, E**

B **In Praise of Our Fathers and Mothers:**
A Black Family Treasury by
Outstanding Authors and Artists
Compiled by Wade Hudson and Cheryl Willis Hudson
This beautiful anthology includes contributions from many of the big names in children's literature. The stories are very personal, and many seem targeted more at adults than children. $17.95 **AA**

The Dream Keeper and Other Poems
Langston Hughes

Langston Hughes's powerful, beautiful poems are always worth reading, but Brian Pinkney's scratchboard illustrations make this collection especially wonderful and accessible. $7.99 **E, M**

Seth and Samona
Joanne Hyppolite

Fifth-graders Seth and Samona couldn't be more different: Seth is quiet, from a strict Haitian family; Samona is always thinking of crazy schemes. She even wants to make friends with Seth's crazy neighbor, Mrs. Fabyi, and, even worse, she wants to enter the Little Miss Dorchester pageant. Seth is always trying to get Samona to stop being so wild, but he usually ends up along for the ride on her adventures, most of the time pleasantly surprised with how they turn out. Samona even triumphs in the pageant; she shows up in beautiful African clothing, good-naturedly teaching everyone a lesson about culture and beauty. Both boys and girls will enjoy this funny, fast-paced story. $3.99 **E, M**

 ### I See the Rhythm
Toyomi Igus

Outstanding paintings by Michelle Wood and a poetic text capture the history and movement of African-American music from the time Africans were kidnapped as slaves, through the Blues, Jazz, Hip Hop and the many other stages of the Black musical tradition. A great book to read aloud and catch the rhythm of the words, with the colorful and exciting paintings. $15.95 **E**

 ### The Wagon
Tony Johnston

The narrator of this book is a young slave boy. The story begins in the days leading up to Emancipation, examines how it feels to be part of a newly free family and ends with the assassination of Abraham Lincoln. $5.95 **E**

I Have a Dream

Dr. Martin Luther King, Jr.

This is the famous speech in its entirety, illustrated by 15 different Coretta Scott King honor or award artists. The cover by Leo and Diane Dillon is beautiful, and the artists all have contributed work that befits this uplifting call to action. $16.95 **E, M**

Wilma Unlimited

Kathleen Krull

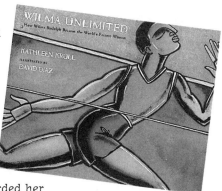

"No one expected such a tiny girl to have a first birthday," begins the story of Wilma Rudolph, one of the greatest athletes of the century. Wilma was born in 1940, one of 22 children. At the age of five, she was stricken with polio; doctors said she would probably be paralyzed for the rest of her life. She discarded her leg braces at age 12, was playing championship basketball by high school, and at 20 won three Olympic gold medals. Her amazing story is accompanied by Caldecott medal winner David Diaz's beautiful illustrations. $6.00 **E**

True North

Kathryn Lasky

Afrika is helped out of her plantation by Harriet Tubman but must find her way to Boston alone, from "station" to "station" on the Underground Railroad. There she meets Lucy, a child of a prominent Boston family, who has recently discovered her beloved grandfather's involvement with the Abolitionists. When Lucy's grandfather dies, Lucy and Afrika must bravely find a way out of Boston, where it has, in 1858, become too dangerous for fugitive slaves. *True North* is a very exciting story and includes a lot of interesting information from the author's research into Boston and runaway slave experiences in the 1850s. $4.99 **M**

The Great Migration
Jacob Lawrence

This book is actually a collection of the great painter Jacob Lawrence's work documenting the migration of African Americans from the South to the cities of the North during and after World War One. The text lyrically describes the conditions of life during the trip and after arrival in the North. $7.95 **E, M**

What a Truly Cool World
Julius Lester

God has just created the world, and it's nice, but dull, so he calls in Shaniqua, the angel in charge of everyone's business, his secretary Bruce, and his wife, Irene God, to shake things up a little. Together, they create colors, bushes, tears and music, and the world becomes the truly cool place it is today. Bright illustrations complement the funny dialogue and nonstop action of the story. $15.95 **E**

Tree of Hope
Amy Littlesugar

This picture book was inspired by Orson Welles's staging of an all-black Macbeth in Harlem during the Depression. Florrie's father is a former actor whose greatest wish is to return to the stage. When the Lafayette Theatre is reopened under the Federal Theater Project, his prayers are answered, and the community is energized during those hard economic times. $16.99 **E**

Happy Birthday, Martin Luther King
Jean Marzollo

The scratchboard and pastel illustrations by Brian Pinkney make this book a unique resource. The text is appropriate for a very young child and explains why we celebrate Martin Luther King's birthday, in language a preschool child will easily grasp. $15.95 **P**

B **Sidewalk Story**
Sharon Bell Mathis
Lilly Etta's best friend and her family are being evicted from their apartment, with no recourse and nowhere to go, their belongings left on the sidewalk. Lilly Etta has few resources except her own determination and intelligence, which she uses to locate a reporter interested in the story of her friend's family. $4.99 **E**

A
B **The Dark-Thirty**
C Patricia McKissack
"Southern Tales of the Supernatural" is the subtitle of this wonderful book, but that tells only part of the story. These original tales are all inspired by African-American history. Meant to be told in the half-hour before nightfall, these stories are mesmerizing. One tells of the haunting of a KKK member who lynched a black veterinarian, another of a young woman's visit to a bus driver who had denied her access to the bus ride that would've saved her baby. All deal with the realities of African-American struggles as well as the supernatural elements of traditional ghost stories. $4.99 **E, M**

B **Run Away Home**
C Patricia McKissack
Sarah Crossman is the only person to glimpse a runaway from a train taking Apache prisoners to a reservation. She later sees the boy sneak into her barn. He is very ill, and she and her mother nurse him back to health. The time is Reconstruction in the South, and many black families are threatened with violence if they assert their rights to economic and political freedom. As Sky, who has lost his parents, becomes attached to Sarah's family, his special skills as a warrior and as a respected member of his people are vital to their survival. The author's Native-American ancestor, and the story of his arrival in the family, inspired this book. $14.95 **M**

The Black Snowman

Phil Mendez

Jacob's mother and little brother are looking forward to Christmas, but Jacob knows his family cannot afford many presents. Lately all he can think about is how much he hates being poor and having dark skin. Then he and his brother build a snowman, and find a brightly colored Kente cloth in the trash to put around his neck. The snowman begins to talk and helps Jacob learn to be proud of his color and his African heritage. $5.99 **P, E**

Zora Hurston and the Chinaberry Tree

William Miller

Zora Hurston's mother taught her that she could do anything and told her many stories from Africa. She encouraged her to explore and pay attention to the human and natural life around her. When her mother died during Zora's childhood, she was able to hold on to her mother's belief in her and her ability to "never stop climbing. ...always reach for the newborn sky, always jump at the morning sun." $6.95 **E**

Uncle Jed's Barbershop

Margaree King Mitchell

Sarah Jean's favorite uncle, kindhearted and determined uncle Jed, is the only black barber in their rural county in the 1920's South. Uncle Jed cuts hair all around the county but dreams of owning his own shop. Sarah Jean recounts how Jed pays for her lifesaving operation with his savings, loses his money again during the Depression and finally gets his own shop—at the age of 79!
$5.99 **P, E**

Freedom Songs

Yvette Moore

In 1963, 14-year-old Sheryl wants more than anything to be popular at school. When she travels south, she sees the reality of segregation and returns home to Brooklyn with a newfound maturity and understanding of the world. She organizes a concert to benefit workers against racial injustice. $4.99 **M, Y**

D **Habari Gani? What's the News? A Kwanzaa Story**
Sundaira Morninghouse
Beautiful paintings by West Coast artist Jody Kim complement this
story of Kia's family celebrating Kwanzaa, with each day's activities
illustrating the principle for that day. This holiday has meaning for
us all, celebrating such principles as *umoja* (unity), *ujima* (collective
work and responsibility) and *kuumba* (faith), but especially for Black
Americans, whose people have created this holiday.
$14.95 **E**

A **Brown Angels**
B Walter Dean Myers
C Myers collected photographs of black children taken nearly 100
years ago and has made an album, using the pictures and original
poems. The photos just begin to tell the stories, but it's easy to look
at this book many times and wonder about the children whose
images are captured from long ago. $5.95 **AA**

A **Harlem**
B Walter Dean Myers
C This book-length poem is the deserving winner of both the Coretta
Scott King Award and, for the magnificent collage art by
Christopher Myers, the Caldicott Honor. The artwork conveys the
range of activities taking place in Harlem, from the late night
music, to the store-front churches, from the despair of some folks
hanging out on the stoops, to the exuberant street life of the young
people. $19.95 **AA**

B **Me, Mop and the Moondance Kid**
C Walter Dean Myers
Fourth through sixth graders will laugh as they read about T.J,
Moondance and Mop's efforts to get Jim and Marla Kennedy, their
Little League coaches, to adopt Mop (Miss Olivia Parrish). Myers
provides good female role models and gently pokes fun at T.J.'s sex-
ist notions. $4.50 **M**

B **The Young Landlords**
Walter Dean Myers
In an excellent story, six kids get involved in neighborhood improvement and suddenly find themselves the owners of a building in their Harlem neighborhood. These teens are good kids, but they don't know the first thing about fixing stopped up toilets and many more of their new duties. A funny and often moving read. $4.99 M, Y

B **Won't Know Till I Get There**
Walter Dean Myers
Steve's parents decide to adopt a streetwise 13-year-old. When Steve and company get in minor trouble, they have to do community service with a group of independent and interesting elders. Good portrayal of adoption of an older child. $4.99 M

A
B **Rosa Parks: My Story**
Rosa Parks
Rosa Parks is a name well known to most schoolchildren for her act of courage on a bus in 1955, but that act was just part of a life dedicated to civil rights and justice for all. $4.99 E

A **Dear Mrs. Parks: A Dialogue with Today's Youth**
Rosa Parks
Rosa Parks is still going strong at 83 years old. She continues to inspire young people who learn about her bravery and important place in history. This book contains letters from young people to Rosa Parks and her timely and thoughtful answers to all kinds of questions; she addresses many issues like why she attended the Million Man March, why bother go to school, how it feels to be 83 and how young people can improve our society. $8.95 E, M

A
B
C **Alvin Ailey**
Andrea Davis Pinkney
Pinkney traces Ailey's life, from his early childhood in rural Texas, to his first glimpse of the great dancer Katherine Dunham in Los

Angeles, to the beginnings of his New York dance company.
Beautiful paintings accompany this biography of an exceptional
man. $4.95 **E**

Hold Fast to Dreams
Andrea Davis Pinkney

Twelve-year-old Deirdre Willis and her family move to an all-white
suburb when her father follows his dream of a high-paying job.
Dee has always enjoyed her Baltimore neighborhood and anticipates
the worst about her new school. A white suburban school is very
different from her old city school, and Dee faces many challenges.
However, she is strengthened by her photography and her knowledge of African-American culture, particularly the poetry of
Langston Hughes. $4.50 **M**

Seven Candles for Kwanzaa
Andrea Davis Pinkney

Kwanzaa is beautifully explained and illustrated in this book. The
seven principles are clearly set out, as well as the other traditions.
This is a great introduction, even for very young children.
$14.99 **P, E**

Kwanzaa
A. P. Porter

The vocabulary, history and rituals of Kwanzaa are all presented in
this well-illustrated and organized book. The social and political
roots of the holiday are woven in throughout the book. $5.95 **E**

Books by

Faith Ringgold Faith Ringgold is an outstanding
artist: her story quilts representing her life and different episodes
in black history have been exhibited and highly acclaimed around
the world. In some of her books, she has taken parts of her quilts
and transformed them into stories for children. Her picture books
are great for all children older than young preschoolers.

Aunt Harriet's Underground Railroad in the Sky

In Cassie's second trip to the sky after her foray upward in *Tar Beach*, she encounters the railroad driven by Harriet Tubman. Ringgold's words and artwork present a unique and creative look at the Underground Railroad though the eyes of a modern black child following the trail. $5.99 **E**

Bonjour, Lonnie

One day, Lonnie wakes up in the orphanage to find a bird who will eventually lead him to Aunt Connie and Uncle Bates, his future adoptive parents. But first Lonnie is led on a magical journey, where he discovers who his parents and grandparents were. His grandfather was a black serviceman who served in France in World War One and later immigrated there to find opportunities denied to him in the United States. His father was killed fighting the Nazis in World War Two, and his Jewish mother gave him to a student at the Sorbonne to bring out of Paris during those dangerous times. This book shares some fascinating history while telling a moving story. $15.95 **E**

Counting to Tar Beach

"We're having a picnic on tar beach, what shall we bring?" This board book about a picnic on the roof is a great way to introduce Faith Ringgold's beautiful artwork to younger kids. $6.99 **P**

Dinner at Aunt Connie's House

Melody has always enjoyed visiting her Aunt Connie and Uncle Bates at the annual dinner and the showing of her aunt's latest art-work. This year is extra special, though, because her aunt and uncle have adopted a son, Lonnie, who becomes Melody's great friend. In addition, her aunt has painted a series of paintings of great African-American women; when Lonnie and Melody enter the gallery, the paintings speak to them with their unique and inspiring stories. $4.95 **E**

B **If a Bus Could Talk: The Story of Rosa Parks**
"This morning a strange-looking bus pulled up at my stop. It didn't look anything like my usual bus...," begins the young narrator of the newest Faith Ringgold story. This is no ordinary bus: as soon as Marcie gets on, it begins talking to her, and she finds out that today is Rosa Parks's birthday, and that this is the very same bus on which Rosa Parks courageously refused to give up her seat. Superb illustrations accompany a simple but interesting and powerful telling of one of the most important stories around. $17.99 **M**

A **The Invisible Princess**
Mama and Papa Love, slaves on the plantation of the cruel Captain Pepper, give birth to a beautiful baby girl. Before Captain Pepper has a chance to steal their only child, the baby is made invisible and whisked away by the powers of nature. She will come again and save her parents from separation, eventually leading the slaves to freedom. With the blind daughter of Captain Pepper, the invisible princess even helps the slave owner find redemption. A blend of history, myth, imagination and hope for peace and freedom for all. $18.00 **E**

B **My Dream of Martin Luther King, Jr.**
Faith Ringgold tells King's story in the form of a dream, which follows the great Civil Rights leader through many different episodes in his life. Ringgold again captures our imagination, even with a story told so many times already. $6.99 **P, E**

A **Tar Beach**
B Ringgold has taken one of her most popular and enchanting quilt
C paintings and turned it into a picture book. "I will always remember when the stars fell down around me and lifted me up above the George Washington bridge," begins Cassie's story, a combination of fantasy and the author's memories of her childhood in Harlem. $6.99 **P, E**

xxxx

Adventures of High John the Conqueror

Steve Sanfield

High John was the folk hero created by enslaved African Americans. John generally gets the best of his master; most of these stories are very funny. Kids will enjoy predicting how John will outsmart everyone this time. $8.95 **E**

Minty: A Story of Young Harriet Tubman

Alan Schroeder

This is the finest of many children's books written about this great American. The illustrations are Jerry Pinkney's wonderful work, and the story of a young girl determined to escape from slavery will surely ring true for all readers. $16.99 **P**

Bicycle Rider

Mary Sciosca

Marshall Taylor was the first black cyclist to integrate the professional bicycle racing circuit. This book is a fictionalized account of Taylor's early years and how he became a bicycle racer and toured around the country and in Europe and Australia. $3.95 **E**

Down in the Piney Woods

Ethel Footman Smothers

Annie Rye is the author's childhood name, and this book is based on memories of her life as the daughter of a Virginia sharecropper. Ten-year-old Annie Rye is happy with her life, and she dreads three stepsisters moving to her home. $4.99 **M**

Families: Poems Celebrating the African-American Experience

Illustrated by Dorothy and Michael Strickland

This book is a collection of short poems addressing many different life and family experiences of African-American children. The poems are by a wide variety of poets, and they are all short. Their length and the picture book format make this book accessible to younger readers. $7.95 **P, E**

Down Home at Miss Dessa's
Bettye Stroud

The narrator and her sister spend a day with their beloved next-door neighbor, Miss Dessa. The girls fix her glasses, help her with the quilt she is making, dress up in her clothes, listen to her stories and dance to her records. A beautiful book about the many ways the very young and very old can learn from and take care of each other. $14.95 **P**

I Love My Hair!
Natasha Anastasia Tarpley

Every night before Keyana goes to bed, her mother combs her hair and tells Keyana how lucky she is to have hair that can do so many things, spin into soft yarn or stay in straight rows or surround her head like a globe. Keyana is adorable, and this book is a fun read for young kids. $14.95 **P**

Front Porch Stories at the One-Room School
Eleanora E. Tate

On a hot, humid night, Margie and her cousin listen to Margie's dad tell wonderful stories of the history of their small town. The stories are great for reading aloud and evoke the feeling of rural life. $3.50 **P, E**

Secret of Gumbo Grove
Eleanora E. Tate

Raisin's interest in history leads her to research the history of the black community in her town. With the help of the church secretary, she uncovers secrets some people would prefer remain hidden. $4.99 **M**

Thank You, Dr. Martin Luther King
Eleanora. E. Tate

Mary Eloise is clearly confused about many things; the messages she gets from television and her fourth-grade teacher are that white is better. When she gets the narrator part in a black history play, she is angry. With the help of her mother, her teacher and two storytellers who visit her school, she begins to understand the richness and importance of her own heritage. $4.95 **M**

Books by

Mildred Taylor writes beautifully about life in the Depression-era South. She explains the importance of her work in her 1977 Newbery Award Acceptance Speech: "Without understanding that generation and what it and the generations before it endured, children of today cannot understand or cherish the precious rights or equality which they now possess...if they can identify with the Logans, who are representative of...many black families who faced adversity and survived, then perhaps they can better understand and respect themselves and others."

Song of the Trees

Introducing Cassie Logan. This is a story about the importance of the land for Cassie's family, who live in the pre-Civil Rights south. $3.99 **M**

Roll of Thunder, Hear My Cry

Classic novel of the effects of racism on Cassie and her proud, independent family. Cassie discovers, among other things, that her school is using cast-off books from the white schools. $3.99 **M**

MILDRED D. TAYLOR
Roll of Thunder, Hear My Cry

Let the Circle Be Unbroken

A further look at the hardships and joys of life for Cassie and her family during the Depression. The cruelty and life-shattering injustice of a racist society is something we need never forget, and Taylor's superb writing and her memorable characters stay with the reader for a long time. $4.99 **M**

The Road to Memphis

In her final year of high school, with the nation on the verge of entering World War Two, Cassie is caught in several dramatic episodes, which culminate in one of her closest friends fleeing Mississippi after injuring three white youths. As in all her books, Taylor combines a powerful indictment of white racism with the stories of Cassie and her family's incredible strength in the face of that racism. $4.99 **M**

The Well : David's Story

Cassie's father tells a story from his childhood in Mississippi in the early 1900s. During a severe drought, the Logan family controls one of the only water sources in their rural area and shares with blacks and whites alike. Unfortunately, some of the Logans' white neighbors react in racist, violent ways to having to accept charity from a black family. $14.99 **M**

xxxx

The Real McCoy

Wendy Towle

The expression "the real McCoy" actually derives from the inventor Elijah McCoy's design for a locomotive lubricating device. The early difficulties of finding a job as a black engineer were finally overcome by his creative talents as an inventor. $4.95 **E**

Have a Happy...

Mildred Pitts Walter

Chris is dreading his Christmas/ birthday, knowing he won't get the bicycle he so badly wants because his father is unemployed. Thanks to his uncle, who encourages the family to celebrate the seven-day festival of Kwanzaa, Chris is busy making special presents for the holiday. The final surprise makes it a Kwanzaa celebration to remember for a long time. $3.99 **E**

Freedom's Gifts: A Juneteenth Story

Valerie Wesley

Juneteenth, the anniversary of the day in 1865 when Texan slaves heard they were free, has always been one of June's favorite holidays. But her cousin Lillie, visiting from New York, thinks the whole thing is stupid. June is ready to give up on Lillie, until a story from Aunt Marshall, a former slave, makes both girls remember the importance of what they are celebrating. $16.00 **E**

Working Cotton

Sherley Anne Williams

Sherley Williams recalls her own experiences as a migrant child in the fields of Fresno, California, in this picture book. We follow her family from their arrival in the fields before dawn, through the long, arduous day, until the family leaves for the bus in the evening. A child's view of a life still lived by many, and of the love and respect she feels for her family. $14.95 **P, E**

Like Sisters on the Homefront

Rita Williams-Garcia

When 14-year-old Gayle becomes pregnant for the second time, her mother takes charge. After arranging for an abortion, she packs Gayle and her baby off to live with her aunt and minister uncle in the south. Gayle must live with her straight-laced cousin and follow strict house rules. As she comes to know Great, the family matriarch, she begins to understand more about her place in her family and in the world. $4.99 **Y**

Books by

Jacqueline Woodson is a wonderful feminist author whose young adult and middle grade books are all beautifully written and provide insight into current debates about race, class and sexuality. Her books almost never play to stereotypes and always open the door for interesting discussion of important issues.

A
B
C
From the Notebooks of Melanin Sun

Melanin Sun, Mel to his friends, is the 13-year-old son of a single mother who is attending law school and finding herself. Mel and his mother have always been close, but when his mother reveals that she is in love with a white woman, Mel's world seems to fall apart. Woodson deals sensitively and wisely with the many issues she raises here. $3.99 **M**

A
B
C
Miracle's Boys

This timely novel introduces three brothers keeping their family together in the wake of the deaths of both of their parents, and the associated guilt and anger. The middle boy has arrived home from a detention center where he spent two years, as a hardened and different boy. The effects of jailing young people can be devastating, and this book is the story of the beginning of his recovery and re-learning how to feel and break down his tough-guy persona. $15.95 **M**

A
Last Summer with Maizon

In a terrible summer, Margaret and Maizon's friendship is tested and stretched. Margaret's father dies, then Maizon is offered a scholarship at a Connecticut private school. These talented and loyal friends will stay with the reader a long time. $3.99 **M**

A
B
C
Maizon at Blue Hill

Maizon leaves her best friend Margaret to attend Blue Hill, an exclusive boarding school where she is one of the only black students. A fascinating look at how one young girl reacts to her first experience in a wealthy, mainly white environment. Maizon's decision to leave Blue Hill is a thought-provoking one. $3.99 **M**

A
B
Between Madison and Palmetto

Margaret and Maizon are back together on Madison Street and in a new school. There are changes as their neighborhood gentrifies, including a friendship with Caroline, a white girl. $3.50 **M**

B **The Dear One**
A terrific look at teen pregnancy, as 12-year-old Feni's mother
agrees to take in a 15-year-old pregnant daughter of an old friend.
The tensions and gradual understanding between the girls, and
Rebecca's eventual decision to give up the baby for adoption, make
this an interesting read. $3.99 **M.Y**

B **A Way Out of No Way**
Jacqueline Woodson, ed.
Stories by many wonderful African-American authors are collected
here, authors who inspired Woodson, a writer herself, when she
was growing up. Some of the stories are fiction, some nonfiction,
but all are about the experience of growing up black in America.
Includes works by James Baldwin, Toni Morrison, Langston
Hughes, Nikki Giovanni and Jamaica Kincaid. A good introduction
to some of the greatest writers of this century. $4.50 **M, Y**

xxxx

A **Cornrows**
B Camille Yarbrough
Yarbrough shows us the historical and cultural significance of
cornrows in the form of a story with lovely black and white illustrations. $5.99 **P, E**

P = preschool
E = early elementary
M = middle school
Y = young adult
AA = all ages

Caribbean Region

Coconut Kind of Day
Lynn Joseph

The author writes from her experiences growing up in Trinidad. The paintings and language feel like a soft, warm trip to the Caribbean. $5.99 **P, E**

Running the Road to ABC
Denize Lauture

Six children live in the countryside of Haiti. Every morning they rise before the first light to run to school. They hold their hand-made palm leaf bookbags and run past donkeys, merchandise going to town, jeeps, butterflies and snakes, all in a rush to get to class on time. Colorful acrylic paintings illustrate this memory from the author's childhood. $5.99 **P, E**

My Little Island
Frané Lessac

Lessac's delightful, bright illustrations dominate the story of young boys visiting the Caribbean island where one of them was born. The boy shows his best friend all the exciting, curious and mar-velous animals, plants, foods and other unique sights and sounds of the island. $5.95 **P, E**

The Village Basket Weaver
Jonathan London

Tavio's grandfather is the master basket weaver in his Caribbean village in coastal Belize. He has woven the baskets for the village for as long as anyone can remember, but now he is growing frail.

Tavio has been watching his grandfather work for many mornings, and knows when he must step in and help the older man finish an important project for the village. $14.99 **P, E**

The Faithful Friend
Robert San Souci

Clement and Hippolyte are best of friends in 19th century Martinique. Clement is white, recently from France, and Hippolyte is the black son of a sugar grower. When Clement falls in love with Pauline, her guardian is determined to thwart their union. Their story bears the mark of Africa, Europe and the Americas in its telling, attesting to the mixed heritage of Martinique. Brian Pinkney's illustrations add to the appeal of this tale of a loyal friend. $16.00 **E**

A Taste of Salt
Francis Temple

This powerful, important story is told as a conversation between two teens in Haiti, both Aristide supporters. One is severely injured during the firebombing of Aristide's church and is in the hospital. Both young people have lived lives unimaginable to most American kids, and reading this book will provide insight far beyond what the TV news shows have to say about Haiti's troubles. $4.95 **Y**

Tap-Tap
Karen Lynn Williams

Just as a picture book should, this book transports the reader-listener to the exciting first ride on a tap-tap, one of the colorful, jam-packed minibuses that take people, their goods and their livestock from place to place in Haiti. After a tiring day at the market, the tap-tap is just what Sasifi needs to perk up again. $5.95 **P, E**

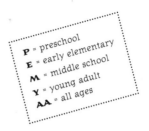

P = preschool
E = early elementary
M = middle school
Y = young adult
AA = all ages

African Heritage and Life

Tales by

Verna Aardema These are well-told, brightly illustrated tales that are popular with kids. **P, E**

Bimwili and the Zimwi
Bimwili is captured by the evil trickster, the Zimwi, in this tale from Tanzania. Of course, she and her village are able to outwit him. $5.95 **P, E**

Bringing the Rain to Kapiti Plain
A repetitive story, great for young readers. It comes from the Nandi people of Kenya and describes how Ki-pat brings down the rain for his herd and all the other animals. $5.99 **P**

Oh, Kojo! How Could You!
This Ananse tale explains why cats are favored over dogs in Ashantiland. $5.99 **P, E**

Who's in Rabbit's House?
Lively Masai Story in which most of the characters are animals represented by traditional designs from African masks. $6.99 **P, E**

xxxx

Kofi and His Magic
Maya Angelou
Renowned poet Angelou and photographer Margaret Courtney-Clarke take us to the West African village of Bonwire, the home of

the colorful woven Kente cloth. In addition to showing us how Kente cloth is made, Kofi takes us on a trip to other parts of Ashanti country. Wonderful book design. $17.00 **P, E**

The Night Has Ears: African Proverbs
Ashley Bryan
Bryan has adapted proverbs from all over Africa and illustrated them with bright, beautifully stylized paintings. The proverbs range from wryly wise ("treat your guest as a guest for two days; on the third day give him a hoe"), to cryptic ("one cannot borrow a man's mouth and eat onions for him"), to prosaic ("patching makes a garment last long"), to beautiful ("no one knows the story of tomorrow's dawn."). $16.00 **P, E**

Mandela
Floyd Cooper
Cooper tells the story of the early life of Nelson Mandela up until the time he was thrown into prison on Robbin Island for 22 years. This book inspires readers, describing Mandela's persistence and faith in the future, despite the cruelty and power of the forces working against the struggle for justice. $15.95 **E**

It Takes a Village
Jane Cowen-Fletcher
Yemi feels great because she is old enough to watch her little brother while her mother sells mangoes at the market. When Kokou wanders off, Yemi's hunt for him leads her to many other adults in the market, all of whom have had a hand in caring for Kokou that day. $15.95 **P, E**

Land of the Four Winds
Veronica Freeman Ellis
The author is from Liberia, and she incorporates elements of the storytelling she grew up hearing into this tale of an African-American boy, Toneih, riding his bike from the local park into a big adventure. He is transported to Liberia, where he uses his strength

and ingenuity to bring color and life back into the land of the four winds. Quite a bit of the dialogue is in a Liberian dialect, but a glossary is provided. $6.95 E

Afro-Bets First Book About Africa

Veronica Freeman Ellis

This terrific introduction to the history of Africa will surprise almost any American adult with new information, yet it is a fun and simple book to read. This book clearly shows the cultural diversity that makes up the vast continent of Africa and focuses on human history rather than big game. $6.95 E, M

The Ear, the Eye and the Arm

Nancy Farmer

This is a totally original book. It takes place in Zimbabwe, 100 years in the future. Three children of a powerful general decide to venture out of their opulent compound and sterile lives. In doing so, they encounter their society head on, from the poorest to the most powerful to those who have gone back to ancient traditional ways. Their parents hire the oddest detectives possibly ever created to locate the children, and the action and interesting details never stop. Contains great information about different aspects of African culture and life. $4.99 M

A Girl Named Disaster

Nancy Farmer

In the bush village in Mozambique where she lives, Nhamo works from dawn until dusk, and is considered a girl of low status due to circumstances of her birth. When she is pledged in marriage to a cruel, old, unhealthy man with two wives, her grandmother encourages her to leave in the night in a boat to try to find her father's family in Zimbabwe. Her journey is harrowing, although she shows herself to be a girl of remarkable courage and resourcefulness. When she finally meets people again after her journey, she faces new challenges as well as great opportunity to have a life of her own making. This Newbery Honor book is engaging, fascinating and not to be missed. $4.99 **M**

Moja Means One
Muriel Feelings

Swahili counting book illustrated with scenes of East Africa. Each number from moja (one) through kumi (ten) counts items including musical instruments, animals of the Savannah, market stalls and Mount Kilimanjaro. $4.99 **P, E**

Jambo Means Hello
Muriel Feelings

Alphabet book of Swahili words with detailed and expressive black and white illustrations. $5.95 **P, E**

Zamani Goes to Market
Muriel Feelings

Today at long last Zamani is old enough to join his father and brothers on their journey to the African town market. His enthusiasm is contagious, and his sharing of his thoughts are well rewarded. Nice illustrations by Tom Feelings. $8.95 **E, M**

The Hunter
Paul Geraghty

Jemima is a young girl who is pretending to be a hunter in the African bush. When she stumbles on an orphaned baby elephant, she discovers for herself the way humans impact populations of wildlife. $5.95 **P, E**

Children of Mauritania: Days in the Desert and by the River Shore
Lauren Goodsmith

Portraits of two young people, their family life, schooling, social lives, work and the many other aspects of life in the developing world. $7.95 **E**

A **Waiting for the Rain**
B Sheila Gordon
C Tengo is a black South African worker on a farm that white Frikkie
will someday inherit. They become friendly, but as they grow up
Tengo becomes part of the liberation movement, bringing the con-
tradictions in their lives to a head in a very dramatic moment.
$4.99 **Y**

A **African Beginnings**
B James Haskins and Kathleen Benson
C A proud and diverse cultural landscape covered the African continent before the invasion and looting of the European slave traders,
missionaries and others. This carefully researched and illustrated
book describes some of the educational, technological, social,
artistic, political and cultural achievements of the many civiliza-
tions that flourished on the African continent. While many of
the accomplishments of these kingdoms disappeared when they
were defeated by the Europeans, much of the heritage of Africa
survives in the dance, music, religion and other aspects of life of
the African diaspora. It is important to counter the idea that all
the great ancient historical achievements occurred in places other
than Africa. $18.00 **M**

electronic
Children of Morocco
Jules Hermes
A photo-essay featuring children of this fascinating Islamic coun-
try. $7.95 **P, E**

B **At the Crossroads**
C Rachel Isadora
We can only hope this story evokes a period that is gone forever. In
it, the children in one of the very poor South African townships
wait for their fathers to come home from the mines. The artwork,
showing the townships' tin shacks and overcrowded conditions, is
a backdrop to the joyful reunion with the fathers. $4.95 **P, E**

Senefer: A Young Genius in Old Egypt
Beatrice Lumpkin
This unique book takes a look at what childhood may have been like for Senefer, one of ancient Egypt's greatest mathematicians. This ancient African child, life in Egypt 3,500 years ago, and the joy of numbers and math make this a great book for any child.
$8.95   E, M

Anansi the Spider
Gerald McDermott
In this classic children's book, Gerald McDermott tells an Ashanti (West African) legend about Anansi the spider and his six sons, named Road Builder, River Drinker, Game Skinner, Stone Thrower, Cushion and Sees Trouble a Long Way Off. Anansi gets in trouble all day long, and each of his sons uses his own special skill to help Anansi out. When, at the end of the day, Anansi sees a globe of light, he does not know which son to give it to. Finally Nyame, the god of all things, steps in and solves the problem by turning the ball of light into the sun. The author's bright, stylized illustrations are perfect for this lively story. $5.95   P

No More Strangers Now: Young Voices from the New South Africa
Tim McKee
Twelve South African teenagers from all racial backgrounds talk about their experiences under Aparthied, what has been happening since the revolution in their country and in their lives, and their hopes for the future. These teens have all lived through historic upheaval in their short lives. Some have also experienced the tremendous material deprivations of the old South Africa, and the poverty and inequality that does not just disappear with political change. $10.95   M, Y

A
B
C **The Singing Man: Adapted from
a West African Folktale**
Angela Shelf Medearis
This story, from the Yoruba tribe in Nigeria, tells of Banzar, a man
who has always loved singing. His older brothers choose practical
trades, but Banzar only wants to be a musician; when he persists,
he is cast out of his village. He wanders around, and finally finds
an older man who also loves music and who will teach him more
about singing. When his teacher dies, he meets a rich king who is
impressed with his musical skill and pays him money to perform.
$6.95 **P, E**

B **Too Much Talk**
Angela Shelf Medearis
This funny, engaging adaptation of a Ghanaian tale begins with a
farmer and his talking yam. It only gets sillier, but the story is
great for small children and the illustrations are colorful and
exceptionally beautiful, and based on African themes. $15.99 **P**

A
B
C **My Rows and Piles of Coins**
Tololwa M. Mollel
The Tanzanian author of this book presents a slice of village life in
her home country. The story tells of the huge importance of a bicy-
cle to a family's life, in transporting not only people but goods to
market. $15.00 **P, E**

B **Orphan Boy**
Tololwa M. Mollel
This legend from the Maasai people tells a story of the morning
star, Kiliken. Kiliken comes down to earth as a boy to live with an
old man and help him with his hard life, on the condition that the
man never ask him about his origins. When curiosity gets the best
of the old man, his helper ascends back to heaven, where he lives
today. $5.95 **P, E**

Song Bird

Tololwa M. Mollel

Here, Mollel retells a traditional story from the Zulu and Xhosa peoples of southern Africa. The story features Mariamu, a young girl whose act of kindness to a magic bird is eventually repaid with prosperity for her entire village. Rosanne Litzinger's illustrations are bright and exciting, adding to the appeal of this already wonderful story. $15.00 **P, E**

Ashanti to Zulu

Margaret Musgrove

A magnificent ABC book of Africa, with each letter representing a different African people. Each illustration is a work of art, and the information about each tribe is fascinating. $5.99 **P, E**

Journey to Jo'burg

Beverly Naidoo

Thirteen-year-old Naledi leads her younger brother on a long, dangerous and eye-opening trip to reach their mother working in Johannesburg. This is a readable story that introduces us to the system that existed under Apartheid. $4.95 **E, M**

Chain of Fire

Beverly Naidoo

Naledi is older now, and actively involved in the struggle against Apartheid. She and her family are forced to move from their village to one of the "homelands." A powerful story of betrayal and resistance written by a London-based, anti-apartheid activist. $4.95 **M, Y**

No Turning Back: A Novel of South Africa

Beverly Naidoo

Twelve-year-old Sipho lives on the streets of Johannesburg in post-apartheid South Africa. The book begins when he makes the difficult decision to leave his mother and abusive stepfather. His

adventures among the malunde, the street children of Johannesburg, as well as with a family who adopts him and in the shelter
where he finally ends up, make for a suspenseful, moving read.
$4.95 **M**

In the Rainfield: Who Is the Greatest?

Isaac O. Olaleye

Nigerian author Olaleye retells a story from his native land, including in the melodic text many of the sounds he must have grown up
hearing in storytelling. Rain, Fire and Wind argue about which
element is the greatest. They decide to have a contest to determine
the answer. Each element unleashes great force upon the land, and
of course fire wreaks havoc on people, animals and plants. Wind
cannot extinguish the fire; only the gentle rain has that supreme
power. Ann Grifalconi's artwork is a stunning, original, swirling
collage of cut paper, marbled paper and photographs, and must be
seen. $16.95 **P, E**

Ogbo: Sharing Life in an African Village

Ifeoma Onyefelu

The author is from a Nigerian village, where she grew up part of
an ogbo, or group of age-mates who become a lifelong clan. They
share play and work as children, and as they grow up, they, as a
group, take on new roles in the village. One ogbo might build a
school or a house for a poor family, another might be the problem
solvers for the village. Illustrated with photographs, this is a fascinating portrait of village life. $15.00 **P, E**

A Is for Africa

Ifeoma Onyefelu

Striking photographs of contemporary Africa, including many of
beautiful children, and fascinating yet easy-to-understand text
make this one of the best alphabet books available. $4.99 **P, E**

A
B **Chidi Only Likes Blue: An African Book of Colors**
Ifeoma Onyefulu
The author and photographer was born in Nigeria. Here, she uses
photos and text illustrating different colors to illuminate various
aspects of village life. $14.99 **P, E**

C **Emeka's Gift: An African Counting Story**
Ifeoma Onyefulu
Onyefulu has taken beautiful photos to accompany her story about
life in the village in Southern Nigeria where she grew up. With
each number, she explains a different part of life for Emeka, a
little boy on his way to find the perfect gift for his grandmother.
$5.99 **P, E**

A
B **Beyond Safe Boundaries**
Margaret Sacks
C Elizabeth has grown up in a wealthy, all-white community in South
Africa, but when she visits her rebellious sister Evie in Johannes-
burg, she begins to see the other side of life under Apartheid and
ask questions about her way of life. $4.99 **M**

B **The Day Gogo Went to Vote**
C Eleanor Batezat Sisulu
This story commemorates the first multiracial election in South
Africa, in April, 1994. Thembi's Gogo, her 100-year-old great-
grandmother, has not left the house in years, but the opportunity
to vote for the new government is too important for her to miss.
She has told Thembi about the time before white people came to
her country; now she will make history by being the oldest voter in
her district. This moving book makes South Africa's incredible history accessible to even very young children. $7.95 **P, E**

A
B
C

Mufaro's Beautiful Daughters

John Steptoe

Kindness wins out over vanity and greed in this folktale from the indigenous people of Zimbabwe. The illustrations are breathtaking, based on pre-colonial Zimbabwean ruins. $16.00 **P, E**

O

One Day We Had to Run! Refugee Children Tell Their Stories in Words and Paintings

Sybella Wilkes, in association with UNHCR and Save the Children
The author worked with refugee children who had fled from Somalia, Ethiopia and Sudan and were living in refugee camps in Kenya. We are given an historical overview of each country and a description of the present situation, after which we read the more personal stories in the children's own voices. Some photographs of the children are included, but most of the illustrations are the paintings they have created in the refugee camps. We learn about the cultures the children came from as well as the conditions that forced them to flee. $8.95 **E, M**

A
B
C

Galimoto

Karen Lynn Williams

In a village in Malawi, Kondi decides he is going to make a galimoto, a toy local children make with wire and ingenuity. A realistic and interesting portrait of village life and a determined seven-year-old boy. $4.95 **P, E**

O

Marriage of the Rain Goddess: A South-African Myth

Olivia Wolfson

This story was inspired, in the author's words, by "a fragment of a Zulu myth." When the Rain Goddess can't find a mate she desires from among the gods, she decides to find a mortal partner. Combining expressive artwork with a lyrical text, this story of the marriage of a cattle herder and the rain goddess also introduces the meaning of Zulu bead "love letters," village architecture and some interesting Zulu customs. $6.99 **E**

Latin-American Heritage

> **P** = preschool
> **E** = early elementary
> **M** = middle school
> **Y** = young adult
> **AA** = all ages

Borreguita and the Coyote

Verna Aardema

In this very funny tale from Ayulta, Mexico, a lamb is able to out-smart a coyote who thinks he is pretty sharp! $6.99 **P,E**

The Gold Coin

Alma Flor Ada

When Juan, a thief, discovers that an old woman has a gold coin, he decides to steal it. As he follows her around the countryside, he discovers that she is a healer and a midwife. In the course of his adventures tracking her down, he rediscovers a side of himself that has been long buried. By the end, Juan realizes he is a changed person. $5.99 **P, E**

A Bear for Miguel

Elaine Marie Alphin

This book is unusual. It is in an "I can read" format, but the story is quite moving; it takes place in El Salvador during the war. Maria and her father go to market early one morning in an attempt to trade their meager possessions, including their table, for some badly needed food. While her father is off trying to find work, Maria makes the painful decision to part with her only possession, her stuffed bear Paco, after a young couple tells her that their son has been injured by the soldiers and can no longer run and play. He only wants a stuffed bear, but the couple cannot afford one in the stores. They give Maria food in exchange for the bear, and she travels home with mixed feelings: she knows she has done the right thing, but misses her beloved Paco. This book will make middle-class children think about what one toy can mean to a child who has nothing and what might be more important than things we own. $3.95 **E**

Ⓑ **Carnaval**
George Ancona

The brightly colored photographs of Carnaval in Olinda, a town in northeastern Brazil, pull the reader into the festivities. Olinda's celebration of this Latin-American tradition attracts revelers from around the world—the masks, costumes, music, dance and life-sized puppets reflect the many cultures of Brazil. $6.00 **E**

Ⓐ **Friends from the Other Side**
Gloria Anzaldua

A young Mexican-American girl in a border town meets a boy who has crossed the border illegally with his mother in order to begin a new life in the United States. $6.95 **E**

Ⓐ **Lupita Manana**
Patricia Beatty

Thirteen-year-old Lupita and her brother are forced to travel across the border from their home in Mexico when their father is killed in a fishing accident. They must work to send money to their mother and four young siblings, but first they need to survive the harrowing journey and find relatives they have never met in the state of California. $4.95 **M, Y**

Ⓑ **Journey for Peace: The Story of Rigoberta Menchu**
Marlene Targ Brill

This biography follows Menchu's life from the time she was a hardworking child witnessing the brutality the landowners and the government perpetrated on her family and on her people, the Mayan

Indians of Guatemala, through her fearless political activism, cul-
minating with her Nobel Peace Prize in 1992. She is truly one of the
heroes of our day, and she continues to speak out for justice and a
future where we can all live together in peace. $14.99 **E, M**

Going Home
Eve Bunting
Carlos and his family are heading home to Mexico for Christmas.
Carlos's parents are both farmworkers who labor many hours
each day in the California fields. When they see a happier side of
their parents when they are in Mexico, the children wonder
why their parents are living in the United States, where life is
so hard. $5.95 **E**

Journey of the Sparrows
Fran Leper Buss with Daisy Cubias
After her father, brother and sister are murdered by the government of El Salvador, 15-year-old Maria, her young brother Oscar
and her pregnant sister Julia enter the United States nailed into a
crate in the back of a truck. They join thousands of other refugees
living illegally in Chicago. Despite extreme hardships, they find
love and compassion in their community, and Maria finds strength
in herself. $4.50 **Y**

The Most Beautiful Place in the World
Ann Cameron
Juan lives with his grandmother in the mountains of Guatemala,
working in the town to support them while he dreams of a different
life. While this book is an interesting look at the beauty and poverty of rural life, it does not give the complete picture of the desperate conditions and repression faced by the Guatemalan Indians.
$3.99 **E**

B **Among the Volcanoes**

Omar S. Castaneda

Isabel tries to reconcile the conflicts in her life between the responsibilities of her traditional Mayan life and her goal of becoming a
teacher, as well as some new ideas brought to the village by a
young North American who is trying to help. The author was born
in Guatemala, raised in the U.S., and has returned many times to
study Mayan village life. $4.50 Y

A **Marisol and Magdalena: The Sound of**
B **Our Sisterhood**
C Veronica Chambers

Marisol and Magdalena are both Panamanian Americans, best
friends and from close families. Their friendship is tested when
Marisol's hard-working, single mother sends her to live with
her Panamanian grandmother for a year. She learns much about
her family and heritage that had been out of reach living in
Nueva York. These girls will resonate with young girls of all backgrounds. $14.95 M

A **Tomàs and the Library Lady**
B Raul Colon
C

Tomàs is a migrant worker in Iowa, far from his Texas home. He
loves his grandfather's stories and wants to discover new stories,
leading him to the library. He encounters a friendly, caring librarian, who helps him find books that give him exciting dreams and
stories to tell. When Tomàs and his family go back to Texas, the
library lady and Tomàs have given each other a gift of friendship.
$7.99 E ALSO AVAILABLE IN SPANISH, *Tomàs y La Senora de la
Biblioteca*, $7.99

B **Gracias the Thanksgiving Turkey**
C Joy Cowley

Miguel's dad, a long-haul trucker, sends a gift to his son in New
York City: a turkey to fatten up for Thanksgiving, when he will join
the family for the holiday. Not surprisingly, once the turkey has a

name—Gracias—and once Miguel and the bird have spent time together, Gracias is no longer viewed as a future meal, but as a pet and a welcome member of the neighborhood. $5.99   **E**

Abuela
Arthur Dorros
Rosalba and her Abuela (grandmother) take a walk together in the park and then decide to fly over the huge city of New York. Sprinkled with Spanish words and lovingly illustrated with bright collages, this is a tribute to the multi-ethnic conglomeration that is New York. $5.99   **P, E**   ALSO AVAILABLE IN SPANISH FOR $15.99

Tonight Is Carnival
Arthur Dorros
The illustrations in this book are arpilleras created by a group of women in Peru. A young boy counts the days until his family can go to Carnival, one of the few celebrations that breaks up the hard work of a poor family living in the Andes, work like tending llamas, planting and harvesting potatoes and transporting water. 20 percent of the royalties from this book go to Oxfam America. $4.99   **P, E**

Under the Lemon Moon
Edith Hope Fine
One night, Rosalinda hears noises outside, so she tiptoes out to the backyard—just in time to see a man run away with all the lemons from her beautiful lemon tree. The next day at market, she sees the man, with his wife and children, selling her lemons! Rosalinda is distraught, but she and her wise friend La Anciana devise a magical and compassionate plan to make everyone happy. Rene King Moreno contributes lovely illustrations. $15.95   **P, E**

ß **Out of the Dump: Writings and Photographs by Children from Guatemala**
Kristin Franklin and Nancy McGirr
This book is part of the ongoing project the authors and the children are working on, documenting the lives of these poorest children, who live on the edge of the dump in Guatemala City. The children's words and photographs speak eloquently of the pain and joy they find around them. The photographs have been exhibited in many countries, and the children have used the proceeds to contribute to their families and to attend school, something that would have only been a dream without this project. Proceeds from this book go to the "Out of the Dump" project. $19.00 **E, M, Y**

ß **The Long Road**
Luis Garay
This autobiographical story follows Jose after soldiers come to his small Central American village. He and his mother take the difficult and lonely journey north, eventually to Canada. As the book closes, Jose is adjusting to life in his new home, building his first snowman and playing with his new puppy. $15.95 **E**

0 **Adventures of Connie and Diego**
Maria Garcia
This book is about multicolored twins who try to escape teasing by leaving the community of people and living among the animals. When they learn to be proud of who they are, they decide to return and live among the people again. $6.95 **E**

ß **The Saturday Market**
Patricia Grossman
A brightly colored look at market day, Mexican style. The book follows the many preparations necessary in order to arrive at the market before dawn. $15.00 **P, E**

○ **Fiesta!**
Ginger Fogelsong Guy
This is a bilingual counting book for very young children. Three
children take a basket around their village and buy "dos
trompetas/two horns, tres animalitos/three animals" and more to
fill the pinata for the fiesta. Delightful illustrations make this a
potential favorite for preschoolers. $15.00 **P**

Children of Guatemala
Jules Hermes
A new addition to an excellent series introducing us to a variety of
Guatemalan children from different areas in this scenic and troubled land. The photographs are beautiful, showing how children
and their parents work and live, with a fascinating narrative
describing life in Guatemala. $19.95 **M**

I'm New Here
Bud Howlett
Jazmin Escalante is about to enter school in the United States for
the first time. She has just arrived from El Salvador, but her feelings and experiences could be those of any student entering school
here whose native language is not English. $17.00 **E**

A Handful of Seeds
Monica Hughes
When Concepción lived with her grandmother, they farmed a small
plot, always saving seeds for the next planting. When her grandmother dies, she loses her home and journeys alone to the city,
where she meets a group of children who live around the city
dump. She joins them in their subsistence life, but improves it by
planting the seeds she has brought with her, growing vegetables to
eat and sell. The paintings by Nicaraguan artist Luis Garay convey
Concepción's difficult yet hopeful life. $14.95 **E**

The Golden Flower: A Taino Myth from Puerto Rico
Nina Jaffe

This lavishly illustrated retelling explains how water came into the world—from inside a giant calabaza, a big pumpkin. There are few children's books that tell Taino myths, and this is an excellent one. $16.95 **P, E**

The Circuit: Stories from the Life of a Migrant Child
Francisco Jimenez

Jiminez writes from his own experience growing up in a migrant family; *The Circuit* is a beautifully written collection of short stories that will captivate young children and adults alike. In the first story, six-year-old Francisco and his family illegally cross the border into California. In the rest of the book, Francisco describes his difficult, sometimes heartbreaking experiences as a migrant worker, as well as the loving encouragement he gets from his family and a few special teachers. $15.00 **E, M, Y**

Parrot in the Oven
Victor Martinez

In this award-winning novel, Manuel goes through a difficult 14th year, experiencing his father's sometimes violent drinking following the loss of his job, his initiation into a gang of sorts and other troubles. Through all, he is a caring and thinking person, and his life seems to be improving by the end of the novel. $5.95 **Y**

Felita
Nicholasa Mohr

Felita is a bright, thoughtful eight-year-old. The changes she faces in the story, including a move and her grandmother's illness, open a window to different aspects of Puerto Rican family life in New York. $4.50 **M**

B **Going Home**
Nicholasa Mohr
Twelve-year-old Felita has never seen Puerto Rico, so when her
parents arrange for her to spend the summer there, she is thrilled.
She is surprised to find herself "Nuyorican" to the local kids, but
she ends up with close friends and a new appreciation of nature
and of her elderly uncle. $4.50 **M**

A **The Bird Who Cleans the World and**
C **Other Mayan Fables**
Victor Montejo
Montejo is a Jakaltek Maya from Guatemala who grew up listening
to the stories contained here. Many of them have never been writ-
ten down before, and all are infused with themes important to the
Maya, including creation, nature and mutual respect. $13.95 **M**

C **Abuelita's Paradise**
Carmen Santiago Nodar
Marita's beloved Abuelita has died; now Marita sits in her grandmother's rocking chair and remembers her stories about growing
up in rural Puerto Rico. Abuelita has created a strong link with the
island in her granddaughter just from her word pictures of her
early life. $13.95 **P, E**

O **Kids Who Walk on Volcanoes**
Paul Otteson
What is a day like for children of the volcano country in Central
America? Check out the lives of contemporary children in the
region—how they have fun, work and go to school if the families
can afford it. Excellent photographs throughout illuminate the
wildlife, landscapes and the lives of the kids in this beautiful and
often troubled region. $6.95 **E, M**

O **Life Around the Lake: Embroideries by the Women of Lake Patzcuaro**
Maricel Presilla and Gloria Soto
The women living around this lake in central Mexico have been master embroiderers for many generations. Their works tell the story of life around a formerly productive and pristine lake that has become more and more polluted, forcing the people who had relied on its bounty to change their ways or move away. The embroideries are beautifully reproduced in this book, and the women clearly have their own ideas about how to improve the situation of life around the lake. $16.95   E

A **Too Many Tamales**
B Gary Soto
C In a variation on a familiar story, Maria is certain she has lost her mother's wedding ring in one of the tamales she has helped prepare for Christmas dinner. The oil paintings by Ed Martinez illustrate perfectly the feeling of this family gathering and the surprise of the children when the ring shows up in an unexpected place. $5.95   **P, E**

A **Grab Hands and Run**
B Francis Temple
Felipe, his sister Romy and his mother must flee for their lives from El Salvador's brutal military dictatorship when Felipe's father is murdered. They become refugees and must use every survival skill they possess to come out alive. $4.95   **M**

B **Saturday Sancocho**
C Leyla Torres
Maria Lili and her grandmother manage to make their Saturday chicken stew with only a dozen eggs. How they go to market in their small town, in what is probably the author's home country of Colombia, and get what they need for the stew is a delightful example of how the barter system works. The colorful illustrations make the reader feel like she is at the market too. $5.95   **P, E**

ᛏ **Cuba: After the Revolution**

Bernard Wolf

This book, full of wonderful photographs and information about contemporary Cuba, will be interesting to adults as well as children. The book focuses on 12-year-old Ana Moreira and her parents, who live in Havana. We follow Ana to school, ballet class and parties with friends, and along the way catch intimate glimpses of a unique country at a pivotal moment in its existence. $16.95 **E**

○ **Spirit of the Maya: A Boy Explores His People's Mysterious Past**

Ted Wood

Kin, a boy of Mayan descent living in Palenque, Mexico, has never been especially interested in his father's Mayan arts. His father makes clay figures and hunting arrows, some of which he sells to tourists outside the pyramids at the Mayan ruins. When his grandfather explains to him about a great Mayan king of the past, he becomes interested in seeing the ruins for himself. He decides to go with his father the next day, and we explore the pyramids and other great architectural works with him. The photos are informative both about the current life of Kin and his family and the rich history of the Maya. $16.95 **E, M**

P = preschool
E = early elementary
M = middle school
Y = young adult
AA = all ages

Books in Spanish and Bilingual Books

B Mediopollito/Half-Chicken
Alma Flor Ada
The author has retold this story, told to her by her Cuban grandmother, of the origin of the weathervane. The text is written in both Spanish and English by the author. Mediopollito was born as a half-chicken with an adventurous spirit and a kind heart. Eventually, the wind blew him onto a roof, where he would be forever safe from the cooking pot and free to observe the world.
$5.99 **P, E**

B Prietita and the Ghost Woman/
C Prietita y La Llorona
Gloria Anzaldua
The author has taken the famous Mexican legend of la Llorona, a ghost woman who snatches children, and turned it around, creating a compassionate ghost woman. La Llorona helps Prietita when she gets lost after finding an herb that should help heal her sick mother. The brightly colored pictures complement a unique story.
$14.95 **E**

B Magic Dogs of the Volcanoes/
Los Perros Magicos de Los Volcanes
Manlio Argueta
When Don Tonio the landowner calls in the lead soldiers to kill the magic dogs that protect the people from misfortune, the people call on the volcanoes for help. $6.95 **P, E**

B
C
Angel's Kite/La Estrella de Angel
Alberto Blanco

A young Oaxacan kitemaker dreams about a bell that has mysteriously disappeared from the village church and eventually uses his creative skills to bring back the bell. $6.95 **P, E**

Lucita Comes Home to Oaxaca/
Lucita Regresa a Oaxaca
Robin B. Cano

Lucita lives in the United states, but she was born in Oaxaca, and most of her Zapotec family lives there. At the beginning of her summer visit with her Mexican relatives, she finds their ways unfamiliar and misses home, but soon she begins to enjoy life in Oaxaca and to love her family there. $14.95 **P, E**

Where Fireflies Dance/
Ahi, Donde Bailan las Luciernagas
Lucha Corpi

In the colorful and vibrant folk-art style of many of the Children's Book Press artists, Corpi tells about her childhood in a town in tropical Mexico. The paintings by Mira Riesberg capture the warm nights, the lush vegetation, and the music, storytelling and family love. $15.95 **E**

Pablo Recuerda la Fiesta del Dia de los Muertos
Jorge Ancona Diaz

Diaz's photo essay of a Mexican family celebrating the Day of the Dead is a wonderful introduction to life in Mexico. We see Pablo, his three sisters and his parents busily preparing for this holiday in many brightly colored photos. Also available in English as *Pablo Remembers the Day of the Dead.* $16.00 **E**

A
B
C
Radio Man
Arthur Dorros

Diego and his family are migrant workers, following the growing season from state to state in the western United States and taking

his one constant friend, his radio, along. The colorful illustrations
and Diego's loving family soften his grim life for young children,
but the difficulties of not having a place to call home certainly
come through. $16.00 **E**

Family Pictures/Cuadros de la Familia
Carmen Lomas Garza
The author recounts her childhood in a large Mexican-American
family in Texas. Garza's paintings and words show life through the
eyes of a child who dreams of becoming an artist as well as the
many aspects of life as a Mexican-American child. $6.95 **E**

In My Family/En Mi Familia
Carmen Lomas Garza
Artist Garza has written a second book of memories from her Texas
childhood. She brings the culture of the border to life with her
descriptions, in both Spanish and English, of outdoor dances in the
garden, making empanadas and many other activities. $6.95 **P, E**

Calling the Doves/El Canto de las Palomas
Juan Felipe Herrera
Even among the many brightly illustrated and eye-catching books
about Mexico, this one stands out, with its beautiful illustrations by
Elly Simmons and text recalling the author's childhood as a
migrant worker. His parents worked extremely hard, but he recalls
his mother's songs and poetry and his father's stories. $14.95 **P, E**

The Upside Down Boy/El Nino de Cabeza
Juan Felipe Herrera
When the author was eight years old, his migrant worker parents
felt it was time for their son to attend school, so they moved into
the city, and Herrera entered school for the first time. This lyrcial
and colorful memoir describes some of the experiences of a young,
talented, Spanish-speaking boy encountering the difficulties and

the wonders of school. His family and his new teacher are supportive and excited about the art, music, poetry and other skills he discovers in himself. The illustrations by Elizabeth Gomez are lively
folk-art-style paintings with lots of fun details, like dancing chick-
ens and a flying cow! $15.95 **E**

C La Calle es Libre/The Streets Are Free
Kurusa
This story is told in Spanish and takes place in the barrios of
Caracas, Venezuela. The children have no place to play and must
play in the streets. With the help of a local librarian, the children
organize a march on City Hall to demand a playground. The illustrations of the mothers, the children, the uncaring bureaucrats and
the community give children in this country a real look at how poor
children live in South America. $7.95 **E**
THE ENGLISH EDITION IS ALSO AVAILABLE FOR $7.95.

○ El Cuento de Ferdinando
Munro Leaf
This is the classic story of the peace-loving bull who frustrates the
bull-fighting public. Available in English as *The Story of Ferdinand*.
$5.99 **P, E**

B The Harvest Birds/Los Pajaros de la Cosecha
Blanca Lopez de Mariscal
In a story taken from the Mexican Indian tradition, Juan is a poor
man in rural Mexico. He wants to farm his own land, but has no
resources. When he finally gets a chance to farm, he farms in a
way that puts nature first and is able to be successful despite the
lack of help and support from others in the town. A beautifully
illustrated, bilingual story. $14.95 **P, E**

B A Gift for Abuelita: Celebrating the Day of the Dead
Nancy Luenn
Rosita must think of the perfect gift to give her beloved, recently
departed grandmother on the Day of the Dead. Robert Chapman's
illustrations are amazing collages made with string, wood, other

objects and homemade paper. This simple story is a good introduction to the Day of the Dead and to a discussion about death
in general and the way in which different cultures deal with it.
$15.95   **P, E**

The Story of the Colors/La Historia de los Colores
Subcomandante Marcos
Subcomandante Marcos, the leader of the Zapatista Rebels in
Mexico, here tells the story of how the gods created colors, one by
one. Domitila Dominguez contributes beautiful illustrations to this
interesting tale for young children. $15.95   **E, M**

**The Woman Who Outshone the Sun/La Mujer Que
Brillaba Aún Más Que El Sol**
Alejandro Cruz Martinez
This is a legend from the Zapotec Indians of Mexico. Lucia Zentano
appears in a village with an iguana, flowers and butterflies as her
companions. She keeps to herself, but eventually her difference
from others leads them to drive her out of town. When she leaves,
so does the town's river, and only by welcoming her back can the
town restore it's natural state of balance in nature. Beautiful folk
art illustrations enhance the magical story. $6.95   **E**

My Mother the Mail Carrier/Mi Mama, La Cartera
Inez Maury
Five-year-old Lupita's single mother loves her daughter, her job
and life in general. The lively Spanish/English text and artwork of
their city neighborhood makes this a favorite with young children.
$7.95   **P, E**

Flecha Al Sol
Gerald McDermott
The author tells a Pueblo Indian tale about a boy who was the son
of the sun, and his quest for his father. Brilliantly colored illustrations highlight this tale. $5.99   **P**

○ **La Princesa Vestida con una Bolsa de Papel**
Robert Munsch
The Paper Bag Princess in Spanish! This is the classic anti-fairy tale,
a funny and popular children's book. Girl outsmarts dragon to rescue prince, with a surprising twist at the end. $5.95 **P, E**

ß **La Peineta Colorada/The Red Comb**
Fernando Pico
A young girl and an old woman plot to
help keep a runaway slave out of the
hands of the law in Puerto Rico in the
middle of the 1800s, when slavery was
still legal. The story, with Spanish
text, is wonderfully illustrated and
provides a model of young and
old working together. $7.95 **E**
AVAILABLE IN ENGLISH, $4.95

The Red Comb
Illustrated by María Antonia Ordóñez   by Fernando Picó

○ **Margaret and Margarita**
Lynn Reiser
Margaret and Margarita are two little girls
who are dragged reluctantly to the park one day by their
mothers. Margaret's story begins on the left page of each spread,
with her English speech in blue, while Margarita says the exact
same thing in pink Spanish words on the right pages. As the two
girls meet and begin playing together, each girl starts trying out
the other's language. By the end of the story, the pink and blue are
interspersed on each page, and both girls leave the park reluctantly,
already excited about playing tomorrow. This is a wonderful, original format for a bilingual book, and Reiser's bright illustrations
show two spirited girls who are not the least bit scared of a language barrier. $4.95 **P**

B **It Doesn't Have to Be This Way: A Barrio Story/**
No Tiene Que Ser Así: Una Historia Del Barrio
Luis Rodriguez
Rodriguez, author of the classic memoir *Always Running: La Vida Loca*, was a gang member in his youth; he now travels around the country talking with young people in gangs. He wrote this picture book about a bright boy who is lured into a neighborhood gang because he sees no alternative. When his involvement leads to a shooting, he finally understands that he must leave the gang and does have other options. This understanding, along with family support, enable him to stop his dangerous involvement with the gang and turn his attention elsewhere. $15.95 **E, M**

B **Con Mi Hermano/ With My Brother**
C Eileen Roe
Gorgeous watercolor paintings illustrate the story of a young Latino boy and his love for his fun and caring older brother. $4.95 **P, E**

B **Atariba and Niguyona**
Harriet Rohmer
In a bilingual tale from the Taino people of Puerto Rico, Niguyona takes a magic journey to cure his ill friend. $15.95 **E**

B **The Invisible Hunters**
C Harriet Rohmer
Nicaragua's Miskito Indians tell the story of three great hunters who are given the power to always be successful in their hunt when they use traditional hunting methods and provide for their own people. When they break these taboos by selling to British traders and using firearms, they pay a dear price for betraying their customs and their people. $6.95 **E**

B **Uncle Nacho's Hat**
C Harriet Rohmer
Ambrosia's Uncle Nacho attempts to dispose of his old hat, but it keeps coming back to him. This is an allegory about the difficulty of making changes. $6.95 **E**

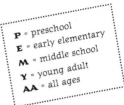

P = preschool
E = early elementary
M = middle school
Y = young adult
AA = all ages

Native-American Heritage

B **The Very Last First Time**
Jan Andrews
Eva, an Inuit girl, takes her first trip alone under frozen ice to gather mussels. Readers will identify with Eva's thoughts and feelings even though her experiences as an Inuit are unique.
$5.99 **P, E**

B
C **Baby Rattlesnake**
Told by Te Ata
An appealing story from a renowned 92-year-old Chickesaw storyteller, this brightly illustrated tale is for all children (and adults) who find their own patience in short supply. Baby rattlesnake learns a valuable lesson in a gentle, loving way. $6.95 **P, E**

A **When Clay Sings**
C Byrd Baylor
What stories do the pots in the desert Southwest tell? Rich in designs from the pottery of prehistoric Native Americans.
$5.99 **P, E**

B **Navajo: Visions and Voices Across the Mesa**
Shonto Begay
Begay is a multi-talented Navajo artist whose paintings and poetry show present-day Navajo life. His book includes poems about memories of his childhood, Navajo traditions and contemporary issues of life on the reservation. $5.99 **AA**

_B_
_C_ **Children of the Midnight Sun:**
Young Native Voices of Alaska
Tricia Brown
The author and photographer profiles eight children representing
different tribes that inhabit Alaska. For each child, life is a unique
mix of tradition and late-20th-century ways. The mix includes isolated village and big city life, and climates from the far north to
the southern tip to the Aleutians. $16.95 **E, M**

Books by
Joseph Bruchac is an energetic Native-American storyteller and educator. He has brought Native-American legends and
their meanings to children all over the U.S., but for those of us in
the Northeast he is particularly relevant, as he has collected stories
from this region, which are harder to find than those of Western
peoples. In addition to these children's books, Bruchac has written
many books for educators.

_B_ **Arrow Over the Door**
This novel for elementary readers is taken from an actual meeting
between Quakers and Native Americans in what is now upstate New
York during the Revolutionary War. Samuel Russell is not sure of
the correctness of his nonviolent faith, as many young men his age
go off to fight the British. Stands Straight, a young Abenaki, feels
justified in his desire to kill Americans, as they killed his mother
and brother. When the Indian war party encounters the silent,
unarmed, Friends Meeting, the encounter is a powerful experience.
Stands Straight sees that these Americans are different, and Samuel
sees for himself that fighting is not always the best strategy.
$15.99 **M**

_A_ **Between Earth and Sky: Legends of**
_B_ **Native-American Sacred Places**
Bruchac has written poems retelling Native-American legends
about ten different sacred places, each in a different region of
North America and sacred to a different tribe. Thomas Locker's

breathtaking oil paintings are a perfect complement to Bruchac's poems about places like the Grand Canyon, Lake Champlain, the Rocky Mountains and Niagara Falls. A map identifying the places and the tribes who inhabit each North American region is included at the end of the book. $7.00 **E**

B Children of the Longhouse

C This novel is set in the 1400s, in a Mohawk village in what is now upstate New York. Eleven-year-old twins tell the elders when they hear a group of older boys led by Grabber planning a raid on a different Native village. The book immerses the reader in Mohawk culture and life in the time before the arrival of Europeans. The game that will become lacrosse, Tekwaarathon, plays prominently. At a major Tekwaarathon game, Grabber tries to hurt Ohkwa'ri, one of the twins, in revenge for his revealing the raid plans. The book is a fast read, as well as a great introduction to Mohawk life. $14.99 **M**

B The First Strawberries

C Here, Bruchac retells a Cherokee story about the first man and woman on earth. When the man sees the woman picking flowers instead of finding food for dinner, he gets angry and yells at her. She runs away, and the man is sorry but cannot catch her to apologize. He asks the sun god to put something so beautiful and tempt-

ing in her path that she will stop running; after several failed attempts, the sun god creates strawberries, which the first woman cannot resist. This engaging story is accompanied by Anna Vojtech's lovely watercolor illustrations. $5.99 **P, E**

The Story of the Milky Way
This Cherokee story of how the Milky Way came to be in the night sky is beautifully illustrated by Native-American artist Virginia Stroud. The book explains why the Cherokee call the great band of stars the "place where the dog ran." $14.99 **P, E**

The Earth Under Sky Bear's Feet
This is a collection of Native-American poems of the land and sky, with magnificent paintings by Thomas Locker illustrating every page. Each poem comes from a different native people from all over the North American continent. $5.99 **E**

Great Ball Game: A Muskogee Story
This legend explains why bats are regarded as animals rather than birds and why birds must fly south for the winter. The illustrations are collages, which work very well for this book. $14.99 **P, E**

Native-American Stories
This is the collection of stories and illustrations, without the lesson suggestions, from the wonderful educational book *Keepers of the Earth*. $12.95 **E, M**

Native-American Animal Stories
The stories and illustrations from *Keepers of the Animals*. $12.95 **E, M**

Return of the Sun
These tales come from the native peoples who inhabited the Northeast woodlands—the area from the Great Lakes east. Bruchac is a master folklorist, and he gives background information on the tribe each tale comes from. $12.95 **E, M**

Thirteen Moons on a Turtle's Back
With Jonathan London
Many Native-American nations have marked the passing of a year by the individual moons, each with its own seasonal character and

connected to the climate and wildlife in a given area. Each of the thirteen moons that makes a year is taken from a different tribal nation, described in clear, poetic language and enhanced by Thomas Locker's magnificent oil paintings. $5.99 **AA**

The Trail of Tears

This easy-reading book packs a lot of history into this format. Bruchac introduces the Cherokees and describes their lives before the United States government forced them from their ancestral home in the Great Smoky Mountains. The Cherokees had a written language, a sophisticated tribal government, and many had succeeded in the "white man's world" before they were rounded up and sent on their dangerous and deadly march to Oklahoma, where most of the Cherokees live today. The suffering of the Trail of Tears makes clear the results of breaking treaties and the greed of the U.S. government, as well as the courage and dignity of the Cherokee people. $3.99 **E**

xxxx

Scholastic Encyclopedia of the North American Indian

James Ciment and Robert LaFrance

This book reflects the revolution in attitudes toward the importance of the past, presenting history as a beacon showing us the way to a more sustainable future. The book includes information about 149 tribes of North America, housing, ceremonies, legends, individual biographies from past and present, and historical information, including how the United States and Canadian governments have continued to this very day in failing to honor treaty obligations. Many of the authors write in the first person about how "Our ideas of progress were different from those of Europeans," etc. $21.95 **E, M**

A **Morning Girl**
B Michael Dorris
C The author gives us a portrait of a Taino family in the Bahamas shortly before Colombus lands. Twelve-year-old Morning Girl and her brother Star Boy take turns telling their very different stories of growing up in a close-knit community, where they live in harmony with the natural beauty of their small island. $4.99 **M**

B **Arctic Memories**
Normee Ekoomiak
Inuit artist Normee Ekoomiak grew up in an area of the James Bay region that was flooded by the first Hydro-Quebec project. His art and text describe both the ancient traditions and the current ways of life for his people in the far north. $5.95 **P, E, M**

A **The Birchbark House**
B Louise Erdrich
C Omakayas, an Ojibwa girl, lives on an island in Lake Superior in the mid-1800s. Her life is a mix of hard work and fun; she picks berries, eats sweets, takes care of her younger brother and has a scary but exciting encounter with a bear. When a stranger brings smallpox to the island, Omakayas and her community are changed forever. Erdrich, the author of many important and wonderful books for adults, contributes her own charming drawings to this captivating and sometimes funny book. $14.99 **E, M**

B **The Star Maiden**
C Barbara Juster Esbensen
The star maiden wants to find a home on Earth. She tries out some forms, but finds in the lake the form she and her sisters will assume. The tale is adapted from one written by the chief of the Ojibway nation in 1850, to preserve his people's heritage. The illustrations are exceptional. $5.95 **P, E**

In the Shadow of a Rainbow
Robert Leslie Franklin
A true story of the relationship between Greg, an Indian from the British Columbia wilderness, and a magnificent wolf named Nahani. $9.95 **Y**

Julie of the Wolves
Jean George
This book is a classic and a Newbury Award winner, about the life of an Eskimo girl. The story begins with her hardships as a child bride and chronicles her flight into the Arctic wilderness and her relationship with the pack of wolves she encounters. $5.99 **M, Y**

Talking Earth
Jean George
Billie Wind, a Seminole, sojourns into the Everglades to find herself and test traditional beliefs in the face of challenges from the outside world. $5.99 **M, Y**

The Goat in the Rug
Geraldine (aka Charles Blood)
Personable Geraldine the goat tells how Glenmae, her Navajo owner, weaves a rug from her wool. Bright, clear illustrations and a simple text explain the value of weavers and weaving in Navajo life. $5.99 **P**

Books by
Paul Goble   Goble is originally from England, but his lifelong fascination with Plains Indian culture has led him to his home in South Dakota and his status as an adopted member of the Yakima and Sioux tribes. All of his books are illustrated with his trademark stylized, colorful, breathtaking illustrations.

Beyond the Ridge
This book is about the spiritual journey of death and can be read on many different levels. $5.99   P, E

Buffalo Woman
A legend based on the importance of the buffalo to the traditional Plains Indians. $5.99   P, E

Crow Chief
This is an ancient Plains Indian story about how the crow became black. The illustrations are Goble's usual magnificent stylized art, and Goble offers a detailed explanation of the story's origin and meaning along with the lively tale. $5.95   P, E

Death of the Iron Horse
One of Goble's greatest books, this is the story of the only time an "Iron Horse," or train, was successfully derailed by a group of Native-American warriors. The perspective is perfect—we actually feel how this invader must have horrified the Native people, belching black smoke and sounding like thunder. $5.99   E

The Gift of the Sacred Dog
Here is the story of how horses came to live with people.
$5.99   P, E

The Girl Who Loved Wild Horses
This legend tells of a girl who feels she is more at home with the wild horses than with her people. After a major storm, the girl is lost with a band of horses for a full year. When she finally reconnects with her people, she realizes she needs to live with the horses, and the people are happy that they have a relative living with the horses. $5.99   P, E

The Great Race
Maybe the most beautiful of all Goble's books, this myth explains how people, one of many creatures, became the guardians of the natural world. $5.99   P, E

The Lost Children

Goble retells a Blackfoot Indian tale about the cost of neglecting children, which is unfortunately a timely theme. Six brothers have lost their parents and are given only the cast-offs of the people at their camp. Only the camp dogs are kind to them. When they finally leave, they decide to become stars in the sky, hoping for kindness from the sun and the moon. Their existence in the sky, as the Pleiades, reminds the Blackfoot to treat every child as a gift from the Great Spirit. $5.99 **P, E**

Red Hawk's Account of Custer's Last Battle

One of Goble's first books, this was written to help young Native Americans feel proud of their history of brave and bloody struggle to resist the onslaught of U.S. colonization. $9.95 **M**

Remaking the Earth

This is a dramatic retelling of the creation story from the peoples of the great plains. Goble has tried to weave together a creation story free of Christian influence, using the remaining fragments of the creation stories from different tribes. $15.95 **E**

xxxx

Thunder Bear and Ko: The Buffalo Nation and Nambe Pueblo

Susan Hazen-Hammond

This book tells the story of the near extinction and reintroduction of the buffalo through the eyes of Thunder Bear, an eight-year-old Pueblo boy. Nambe Pueblo, where Thunder Bear lives, is the site of the relocation of many buffalo, and we learn, along with Thunder Bear, the facts about buffalo as well as their importance in Native American history. The illustrations are stunning photographs of Thunder Bear, Nambe Pueblo, and especially the buffalo who now live there. $16.99 **E**

A **Pueblo Storyteller**

B Diane Hoyt-Goldsmith

The story of Cochiti Pueblo, New Mexico, is told through the eyes of ten-year-old April as she learns traditional activities from her grandparents and other Pueblo residents. Simple but educational, with full-color photographs. $6.95 E

B **Heetunka's Harvest: A Tale of the Plains Indians**

Jennifer Berry Jones

Every autumn, Heetunka, the bean mouse, gathers her beans for the winter. Women of the Plains Indians harvest the beans, but always leave grain in exchange. When one woman decides to harvest the beans and leave nothing for the mouse family, she is punished in such a way that she and we learn that you must give to nature when you take from her. $8.95 P, E

O **Hide and Sneak**

Michael Avaarluk Kusugak

Hide and seek is a popular pastime for children in the far north; parents often warn that an Ijiraq will hide the children who stray too far, and if an Ijiraq hides you, no one will ever find you again. Wonderful paintings with Inuit motifs help us understand what the land and the life are like in this tale of a young girl following her curiosity and coming home again. $5.95 P, E

O **A Promise Is a Promise**

Michael Avaarluk Kusugak and Robert Munsch

Allashua's (from *Hide and Sneak*) first appearance is in a story about ice fishing and how she decides to fish in the sea despite her mother's warning. Allupilluit grabs her but proves no match for her wise mother. A good mix of a contemporary, loving, Inuit family with a fantasy using an Inuit mythical character. $5.95 P, E

β **This Land Is My Land**
George Littlechild
A wonderful book for any young person interested in what it means
to be an artist. Littlechild is an immensely talented artist, and he
shares the insights and inspirations behind many of his works of
art, most of which are about Native-American history, culture and
his personal background as a Plains Cree Indian. The reproductions of his work are all very beautiful. $15.95 **AA**

β **Wilma Mankiller**
Linda Lowrey
This illustrated biography of the former Cherokee Principal Chief
includes background information about the Cherokee and the Trail
of Tears, when the author explains the forces that helped Mankiller
stay strong in the face of her challenging life. When she was a
child, her family moved from Oklahoma, and it was only after 20
years away that she returned to begin her path as leader of the
Cherokee. A fascinating book about a unique and important
woman. $5.95 **E**

β **Children of the Morning Light: Wampanoag Tales**
Told by Manitonquat
The Wampanoag are the Indians of Southeastern Massachusetts,
and Manitonquat is committed to telling the unique tales of his
people. $16.95 **AA**

○ **So Sings the Blue Deer**
Charmayne McGee
Moon Feather is a 13-year-old Huichole Indian boy living in the
Sierra Madre of Northern Mexico. When the Mexican government
offers the Huicholes 20 new deer to try to re-establish the species,
they undertake the difficult journey to the huge metropolis of
Mexico City. This is based on a true story and is a very exciting
tale of the mix of contemporary, ecology and ancient ways of life.
$14.95 **M, Y**

ℬ Crossing the Starlight Bridge

Alice Mead

Rayanne Sunipass has always lived on an island off the Maine coast in a Wabanaki community. When her father leaves, she and her mother must move to the mainland to live with her grandmother. She misses her friends, her father and the natural life of the island. Ray's adjustment isn't easy, but knowing she has roots on her island and in her culture helps her look ahead to the day she may return. $3.95   **E, M**

A   Annie and the Old One

ℬ Miska Miles

C Annie learns that the progress of the rug being woven on the family loom foreshadows the death of her beloved grandmother with whom she shares daily tasks, stories and deep affection. Annie schemes to alter the course of impending death, but her wise grandmother guides her toward a greater understanding of the cycle of earthly life. $7.95   **E**

ℬ Owl in the Cedar Tree

C Natachee Scott Momaday

Haske, a young Navajo boy, is torn between two paths, that of a white-man's school and the modern life favored by his boarding school-educated parents, and the traditional customs represented by the stories of his old grandfather. The author, part Cherokee, has spent much of her life teaching on Indian reservations. $9.95   **M**

A Gift Horse

ℬ S. D. Nelson

Flying Cloud, a Lakota boy, receives a horse for a present at the beginning of this book and has many adventures with this horse during the long process of becoming a Lakota Warrior. The story is based on the author's imagining his grandfather's life. His own bright illustrations detail the story. $14.95   **E**

Forbidden Talent
Redwing T. Nez

Ashiki is a Navajo boy living on the reservation with his grandparents. His calling is art: he draws wherever he is, even painting his sheep and his horse. His grandfather feels at first that he should only make art in the Navajo way, but eventually he gives in when he sees that Ashiki must use his gifts, and he slowly comes to appreciate his grandson's skills. This book is based on the author's childhood, and his paintings are the illustrations. $14.95 **E**

Native-American Sign Language
Madeline Olsen

This book contains dozens of signs that Plains Indians used when they encountered a tribe that spoke a different language, or when silence was of value. The language is quite sophisticated, and the illustrations are clear and interesting. In addition, the signs are grouped in sections, with information about family, food, time, etc., and how these related to the Plains Indians. $4.95 **E, M**

Did You Hear the Wind Sing Your Name?
An Oneida Song of Spring
Sandra De Coteau Orie

The author is an Oneida poet; she shares with us the excitement she feels about the natural world in the spring. The artwork by Christopher Canyon is striking and inviting. $6.95 **P, E**

The People Shall Continue
Simon Ortiz

This is probably the best overview of Native-American history for kids. This book makes it clear that Native people have been the victims of a brutal conquest, but it also leaves the reader with hope for the future. $6.95 **E, M**

Grandchildren of the Incas
Matti Pitkanen

In a photo-essay about the modern-day Quechua people of Bolivia and Peru, we also learn much about their ancestors, the Inca. The text and photos show a people who are trying to hold on to their proud, ancient culture and survive in the less-than-ideal conditions of the modern world. $6.95 **E, M**

B
A, B, C's the American Indian Way
Richard Red Hawk
From the beautiful photograph of a young Indian girl from the Northwest on the cover through the drawing of a Zuni Pueblo, each letter is illustrated by an historical figure or a cultural symbol for a tribe, such as a Kachina symbol or a tipi. $6.95 **P, E**

C
Ahyoka and the Talking Leaves
Peter and Connie Roop
Ahyoka and her father, Sequoyah, are remembered through history for their development of a written Cherokee language. A fascinating, easy-to-read story taken from actual history. $4.95 **E**

B
C
Home to Medicine Mountain
Chiori Santiago
Based on artist Judith Lowry's father and uncle's childhood experiences in the harsh environment of the government's schools for Indian children, this is painful historical reminder of our not-so-distant past. The government wrenched these children from their homes to "help" them unlearn their Indian ways, and didn't even send them home in the summer. The two brothers rode the rails home in the 1930s and made it from Southern California home to the Sierras for a summer of family and renewal. $15.95 **E**

B
People of the Breaking Day
Marcia Sewall
The full color paintings and poetic language of this book show the lives of the Wampanoags before the arrival of the Europeans in North America. Includes a glossary of Wampanoag words and terms. $5.99 **E**

Native Dwellings Series

Bonnie Shemie

The books in this fascinating series contain beautiful artwork and lots of detail. Each book focuses on one type of dwelling commonly built in an area of North America and talks about why and how they are built as well as the lives of the people who live in them. $6.95 **E**

Houses of Bark: Tipi, Wigwam and Longhouse—The Woodland Indians

Houses of Hide and Earth—The Plains Indians

Houses of Snow, Skin and Bones— The Far North

Houses of Wood—The Northwest Coast

Giving Thanks: A Native-American Good Morning Message

Chief Jake Swamp

The words in this book are based on the Thanksgiving Address, an ancient message of peace and appreciation of Mother Earth and all its inhabitants. Children, too, are taught to greet the world each morning by saying thank-you to all living things. According to Native-American tradition, people everywhere are embraced as family. The illustrations are beautiful landscapes by painter Erwin Printup, Jr. $5.95 **P, E**

C **From Abenaki to Zuni: A Dictionary of
Native-American Tribes**
Evelyn Wolfson
The 68 largest Indian tribes in North America are profiled here,
with line drawings of housing, clothing and arts, as well as maps.
This book is easy to use and full of information about history,
culture, foods and travel both long ago and today. $11.95   **E. M**

C **A Boy Becomes a Man at Wounded Knee**
Ted Wood with Wanbli Numba Afraid of Hawk
Wanbli Numpa is a boy of the Oglala Lakota. His father, uncles and
other riders prepare for and recreate the 150-mile ride that their
ancestors were forced to endure. On the ride, the temperatures
tumble to 50 below, but the determination of the riders to com-
memorate their ancestors' brutal murder keeps them on track. The
book begins with an historical introduction about the massacre at
Wounded Knee and then shifts to Wanbli Numpa's own voice
describing the ceremony, the route, the conditions and the historical importance of the ride. $6.95   **E. M**

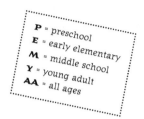

P = preschool
E = early elementary
M = middle school
Y = young adult
AA = all ages

Asian Heritage

Me and Alves: A Japanese Journey
Terumasa Akio

Alves, an exchange student from Brazil, comes to stay with a provincial farm family in northern Japan. We discover the daily life of Hokkaido as we watch Alves explore the island and win the admiration and friendship of many people there, even those who are initially wary of foreigners. $4.95 **E, M**

Halmoni's Day
Edna Coe Berclaw

Jennifer's Korean grandmother arrives just in time to visit her school for grandparents' day. Jennifer barely remembers her grandmother, and can speak little Korean herself, so she is a bit nervous about bringing her traditional grandmother into her classroom. However, when her grandmother tells the class a powerful story about her own wartime childhood, the entire room is engaged, and Jennifer comes closer to understanding her heritage and her grandmother. $15.99 **P, E**

Dia's Story Cloth: The Hmong People's Journey of Freedom
Dia Cha

The author relates her life story, weaving it with that of her people, through words and story cloths, stitched by her aunt and uncle in a refugee camp in Thailand. The story of her harrowing journey from a once-peaceful village in Laos, to a camp in Thailand, to the United States, is inspiring. $6.95 **E, M**

B **China's Bravest Girl**

Charlie Chin

In a legend of ancient China, Hua Mu Lan sees that her father is too
old to answer a call to military service. She convinces him to let
her go in his place, and for ten years distinguishes herself in bravery. When she finally returns home, she is able to command respect
from both women and men, an accomplishment unheard of for
women in Ancient China. $6.95 **P, E**

A **Children of the River**

B Linda Crew

C This excellent young adult novel follows Sundara's life in Oregon
after her escape from Cambodia under the Khmer Rouge. This book
is packed with Cambodian cultural and historical information, but
it is also a wonderful portrait of a strong, intelligent teenager and
her burgeoning love relationship. $4.99 **Y**

A **Buddha**

B Demi

C Siddhartha was born a prince many years ago in a kingdom in
India, shielded by his father from all the world's troubles. He had
great curiosity and sensitivity, and eventually left his life of splen-
dor for a wandering spiritual journey, which culminated in the discovery of his spiritual destiny and Buddhist philosophy. Demi is a
practicing Buddhist; this book reflects her deep understanding of
the story of Buddha. $18.95 **E, M**

B **Happy New Year!**

C Demi

This unique approach to the Chinese New Year brings together
Demi's stylized, colorful artwork with fascinating information.
Each page spread covers a different aspect of the Chinese New Year
such as "Trees and Flowers," "Heavenly Beings" and "Paint and
Parade." The detailed art and text together provide a good understanding of the historical meaning and modern way of celebrating
this 15-day holiday. $6.99 **AA**

ß **One Grain of Rice: A Mathematical Folktale**
Demi
In this classic tale from India, a girl named Rani finds a way to use
the power of mathematics to teach a vital lesson about greed to a
powerful raja, who was hoarding much-needed rice in his store-
houses. After Rani does a good deed for the raja, he asks her what
she will have as her reward. She asks for one grain of rice, to be
doubled every day for 30 days. The raja thinks he is getting a great
deal for his reward payment, until around the middle of the 30
days! This is a great math lesson, as well as a fun tale to read. Demi
has written a number of other books related to Indian art and
culture. Here, as in all her books, the intricate, colorful illustrations
are also her own. $19.95 **E**

○ **Our Journey from Tibet**
Laurie Dolphin
The author follows Sonam, a nine-year-old girl from Tibet, and her
two sisters, during their dangerous and grueling journey with a
group of other children out of Tibet, through the Himalaya, to the
Tibetan Children's Village in Dharamsala, India. Thousands of children have taken this journey during the Chinese occupation of
Tibet. In India, they live at the home-in-exile of the Dalai Lama
and are educated in the traditions of Tibetan culture, something
presently outlawed in their homeland. The importance of culture
and religion to these peace-loving and traditional people is so great
that they willingly undertake this heartbreaking temporary family
separation and difficult journey. The words and outstanding photographs by Nancy Jo Johnson help children understand the horrible
price Tibet has had to pay under Chinese occupation, as well as the
beauty and worth of their traditional way of life. $15.99 **E, M**

A
B **How My Parents Learned to Eat**
C Ina Friedman
A delightful story of the courtship between a young girl's Japanese
mother and her American father. Both young people desire so

much to impress the other that they each learn to master the eating
utensils of the other's homeland for their first meals together.
$5.95   **P, E**

The Lotus Seed
Sherry Garland
The narrator's grandmother was only able to bring a lotus seed
with her when she was forced to flee Vietnam during the war.
When the grandson plants the lotus seed, his grandmother is distraught at the loss of her only tie to her old country. When a lotus
blooms, she is able to help her grandchildren understand their
connection to Vietnam. $6.00   **E**

The Mountains of Tibet
Mordecai Gerstein
A woodcutter from Tibet dies and is given infinite choices about
what he will be in his next life. This peaceful man's choice to
return as a young girl may surprise some, but it also makes sense
and inspires discussion and thought. $5.95   **P, E**

Stories from the Silk Road
Cherry Gilchrist
This lavishly illustrated book introduces young readers and listeners
to the path that led to cultural, artistic, religious and economic
changes around the world. In addition to recounting the fascinating history of the Silk Road's route and its travelers, the author
retells folktales from some of the varied cultures along this road
from China to Tashkent. $19.95   **E**

Roses for Gita
Rachna Gilmore
When she lived in India, Gita learned all about flowers and garden-
ing from her grandmother, but now Gita's family has moved to
Canada, thousands of miles away from her grandmother. Gita
misses India, but she becomes fascinated with her neighbor. He is

gruff with her, but she can't stop peeking over the fence at his beautiful garden. When she decides to take the initiative and give her neighbor a gift for his garden with a message, a special friendship is born, helping both Gita and Mr. Flinch out of their loneliness. $5.95 **P, E**

B **Lights for Gita**
Rachna Gilmore
Gita can't believe she has to celebrate the Hindu holiday Divali in cold, gray Canada. She wishes she was back in India with her relatives setting off fireworks long into the night. Just when it looks like this will be the worst Divali ever, Gita learns a lesson about filling the darkness with light from within herself. $9.95 **E**

electronic **Children of India**
Jules Hermes
Wonderful photographs and fascinating text describe the lives of children in some of the many diverse geographic areas and economic situations of India. From a tea seller to a princess, a restaurant worker to a future Buddhist monk, the children Hermes profiles in this book will surprise and fascinate most American kids. $7.95 **E**

A **Hush**
B Mingfong Ho
C This lovely rhyming lullaby written by Thai native Mingfong Ho is based on her own childhood memories of falling asleep to the sounds of green frogs, mosquitoes, water buffalo, creeping lizards, swinging monkeys and many more animal and village sounds. $6.95 **P**

B **Kim/Kimi**
C Hadley Irwin
Kim is the daughter of a white mother and a deceased Japanese father. She journeys to the west coast to find some answers about her Japanese heritage and gets some lessons about history and culture that she never expected. $3.95 **M, Y**

○ **Children in China**
Michael Karhausen
This is not actually a children's book, but an in-depth look at children in different areas of China. The author/photographer highlights many of the problems facing Chinese children, including those of patriarchal customs, urbanization and pollution. However, the photos show happy, healthy-looking children living in a culture that cherishes them and values their education and well-being.
$24.95 **Y**

○ **Grandfather's Dream**
Holly Keller
Keller's experience in a volunteer group of Americans working on saving cranes in Vietnam inspired this moving, beautifully illustrated book. Grandfather dreams of the return of the cranes to his town, although they have been gone since the war. Will the restoration project bring them back? $16.00 **E**

B **Who Belongs Here? An American Story**
Margy Burns Knight
Nary's parents were killed in the war in Cambodia, but he was able to escape with his grandmother. They eventually make it to the United States, where Nary experiences the many aspects of immigrant life in the U.S., including the new security of having enough to eat and the problem of racism at his new school. This book brings up important issues associated with our status as a country of nearly all immigrants. $8.95 **E, M**

B **D Is for Doufu: An Alphabet Book of Chinese Culture**
Maywan Shen Krach
The author presents many facets of Chinese culture, including an explanation of how some of the frequently used characters (written words) were created, and the history and philosophy behind words from jade, to feng shui, to the idea of "I" or "me," to the Chinese Zodiac. The artist Hongbin Zhang has created rich and wonderful work, using the style of Chinese folk art, with a spectacular range of colors and variety. $17.95 **E, M**

◊ A Is for Asia

Cynthia Chin Lee

"A is for Asia, a third of the world," begins this beautiful alphabet book. The book is unusual in that it describes life all over Asia, including Mongolia, Siberia and the Middle East. Yumi Heo's watercolor illustrations are detailed and wonderful; this book is not to be missed. $5.95 **P, E**

⍝ At the Beach

Huy Voun Lee

On a sunny day at the beach, Xiao Ming's mother is teaching him to write Chinese in the sand. She shows the character and then explains the picture-origin of the character. The collage illustrations of a delightful day at the beach provide great ideas for kids to invent their own picture-characters. $6.95 **P, E**

℔ In the Park

Huy Voun Lee

This author has written two other outstanding books with the same goal as this book—creating a visually appealing book, with a simple story, to teach some basic Chinese characters to young children. Xiao Ming and his mother take a walk in the park. While there, her mother explains the origins of the characters for earth, fruit tree, nest, stream and other outside words, and also shows the actual character. This book will be welcome by the many fans of *At the Beach* and *In the Snow*. $15.95 **P, E**

◌ In the Snow

Huy Voun Lee

A young boy and his mother spend the first snowy day of the winter discovering some Chinese characters and learning how they originated. This book and its companions, *At the Beach* and *In the Park*, make a great introduction to Chinese language. $15.95 **P, E**

B **Silent Lotus**

Jeanne M. Lee

In a beautiful, lakeside rural village in ancient Kampuchea, Lotus is born. It becomes apparent that she is deaf, but she is very happy among the graceful shore birds and nobody really sees her deafness as a problem. When Lotus travels with her parents to the city, she becomes enchanted with the dancers at the palace, and her grace and expressive dancing abilities become known throughout the land. The story is inspired by decorations on the temples at Ankgor Wat. $5.95 **P, E**

B **The Song of Mulan**

Jeanne M. Lee

Mulan did not originate with the Disney movie, but with the poem rendered in this book, in both English and in Chinese characters. The poem tells the story of Mulan, who rides off to fight a war, in which all families must provide a father or son. In place of her father, Mulan fights for many years, distinguishing herself with her bravery, and is never revealed as a woman until she leaves the service of the emperor. $15.95 **E**

A **In the Year of the Boar and Jackie Robinson**

B Bette Bao Lord

C This is a wonderful story, a very funny look at Shirley Temple Wong's first year in Brooklyn. The year is 1947 and she has just sailed from China; we really get a feel for the time, the place and immigrant life. $4.95 **E, M**

B **Journey Home**

C Lawrence McKay, Jr.

Mai's mother is one of the Vietnamese children brought to the United States during the war and adopted by an American family. Mai and her mother travel to Vietnam, where her mother attempts to find her birth family. She has little information, but with the unique kite that was left with her at the orphanage, she is able to piece together something about her origins at that war-torn time. Mai and her mother both come away with a new, deep appreciation for their heritage and a feeling that a gap has been closed. $6.95 **E**

April and the Dragon Lady
Lensey Namioka

April Chen is a high-school junior living in Seattle. Her grandmother has always criticized her and favored her brother, but now April is the one who must care for her as she gets older. An interesting look at the contrast between Chinese and American Cultures, this book manages to avoid stereotype in examining the theme of conflict between traditional and modern ways. The story ends with a satisfying, unique twist. $6.00 **Y**

Aekyung's Dream
Min Peak

Aekyung has recently arrived in the United States from Korea and is having a difficult time adjusting to her new life. A dream helps her begin to take pride in her heritage and adjust to her life in America. $14.95 **E**

Turtle Bay
Savior Pirotta

Taro's sister Yuko thinks Jiro-San is strange because he sweeps the beach every day, but Taro likes to follow Jiro-San and learn from him about the wildlife of the bay. One night, Jiro-San asks Taro to wait with him for some special friends. Yuko comes too, and the friends turn out to be sea turtles hatching their eggs on the beach. $15.00 **P, E**

Dragon Kite of the Autumn Moon
Valerie Reddix

Tad-Tin has always spent Kite Day with his grandfather, flying the special kite they build together every year. But this Kite Day finds grandfather sick in bed and Tin without a kite and very sad. Tin

decides to sacrifice his special dragon kite in the hope that it will
aid in grandfather's recovery. Watercolors by Taiwanese artists
Jean and Mou-Sien Tseng help convey the feeling of the countryside
and people of Taiwan. $14.00 **P, E**

○ **People Who Hugged the Trees**
Deborah Lee Rose
An inspiring version of the legend of the original Chipko or "hug
the tree" movement of Rahasthan, India. Beautiful watercolors
depict the strength and determination of Amrita Devi, a woman
who led her community to protect the forest whose shade and wind
protection was so important to their survival. $6.95 **E**

♭ **First Apple**
Ching Young Russell
Ying faces many obstacles in purchasing an apple for her grandmother's birthday gift; they all cost more than she can afford.
But using her spunk, honesty and creativity, she is finally able to
give her grandmother the perfect gift. A fun book for young readers and a good introduction to life in China. $4.99 **E**

♭ **Sachiko Means Happiness**
Kimiko Sakai
Sachiko can remember well when her grandmother was healthy
and an active participant in family life. After a period of anger,
frustration and sadness, Sachiko comes to terms with her grandmother's Alzheimer's disease in this moving story. $6.95 **E**

○ **Two Lands, One Heart**
Jeremy Schmidt
TJ is a seven-year-old boy whose mother was one of the Vietnam
War "orphans." Nineteen years later, TJ's mother, his aunt and his
American grandmother journey to the family farm in Vietnam.
There TJ meets a huge extended family, including his mother's par-
ents, who were separated from their children in the chaos at the

end of the war. The photos and information about life in contemporary Vietnam are beautiful—lots of great shots of TJ getting to know his Vietnamese relatives. $16.95 **E, M**

The Stone Lion
Alan Schroeder

In a story from Tibet, two brothers, one greedy and one generous, are rewarded appropriately by a stone lion on top of a bleak mountain. The paintings convey the beauty and harsh conditions of the setting at the top of the world. $14.95 **P, E**

The Whispering Cloth
Pegi Deitz Shea

In a refugee camp in Thailand, Mai, a young Hmong girl, passes the time stitching pa'ndau and listening to her grandmother and other women in the camp tell stores of times past. Mai's grandmother encourages her to stitch her own story in her next embroidered picture, and Mai does, telling the story of how her parents were killed and she came to live in the camp and of her hope for a better life. The illustrations incorporate the beautiful, hand-stitched pa'ndau. $8.95 **E**

Chinese New Year's Dragon
Rachel Sing

A young Chinese-American girl with a large extended family describes the traditional celebration her family enjoys every year at this important time. Since they are celebrating the year of the dragon, we also get to learn about that ancient and fascinating symbol. $5.99 **E**

Tibet Through the Red Box
Peter Sis

The author's father, a filmmaker, spent over a year in Tibet in the 1950s, sent there by the Czech government to document the building of the road that would bring Chinese troops into Tibet and end their isolation and their freedom. The text of the book alternates between the author's writing and his father's diary about this critical time, always kept in the red box on his father's desk. Sis's father knew nothing about Tibet, and his diary reveals his wonder at all he learns every day he is there, especially focusing on his spiritual growth and discoveries. The artwork is astounding, and on each page is a new revelation. $25.00 **M, Y**

Angel Child, Dragon Child
Michele Surat

Ut is a Vietnamese child who has come to the United States. When she begins her new school, she feels very shy and upset because a red-haired boy picks on her. But when the red-haired boy learns about Ut's life, thanks to a thoughtful school principal, he decides he wants to help Ut and her family think of a way to bring Ut's mother from Vietnam. $4.99 **E**

The Walking Stick
Maxine Trottier

As a boy, Van finds a teak walking stick outside the Buddhist temple where his beloved uncle is a monk. Van and his uncle clean and polish the stick, and he carries it always. When war comes to Vietnam, the stick becomes his link to his homeland, after Van, his wife and his daughter safely leave and come to a Western city. He becomes old, and still walks with his stick, telling tales of Vietnam, and developing a bond with his granddaughter, in whom he sees his youthful self. He gives her the walking stick, which she returns to its resting place, a Buddhist temple in Vietnam. The illustrations by Anouchka Gravel Galouchko are striking, colorful and perfect for this moving story. $15.95 **E**

Little Weaver of Thai Yen Village
Tran-Khan Tuyet

Hien is injured and orphaned during the Vietnam War and comes to the U.S. for treatment. She is adopted, and in her new home she weaves blankets to send back to her people in Vietnam. Bilingual in Vietnamese and English. $14.95 **E**

Books by

Yoshiko Uchida   All of Yoshiko Uchida's books speak
eloquently about the Japanese experience in America. Her characters are inviting and interesting; these books will stay with readers
a long time.

Journey to Topaz
Yuki and her family are forced to leave their San Francisco home
during World War Two for the horror of Topaz, a prison camp in
the Utah desert. $8.95 **M**

The Journey Home
In the aftermath of the camps, Yuki, her family and other Japanese
families try to put their lives back together. With cooperation, hard
work and some helpful neighbors, Yuki's family begins the road to
stability and recovery. $4.95 **M**

Jar of Dreams
When Aunt Waka visits from Japan, Rinko learns valuable lessons
about her heritage and what it means to be Japanese in San Francisco during the Depression years. $4.95 **M**

The Best Bad Thing
Rinko helps a newly widowed friend of her mother's during the
summer in (then) rural Oakland, and learns more than she ever
expected. $4.95 **M**

xxxx

Celebrate! In Southeast Asia
Celebrate! In South Asia
Joe Viesti and Diane Hall
Each of these books is comprised of a two-to-four-page photo
spread and essay about each of the major holidays celebrated in
these regions of the world. A few of the holidays, such as Tet, are

well known here, but the majority are new to us, such as Baishakhi, the Bengali New Year and the Surin Elephant Roundup in Thailand. $16.00 EACH **E**

Judge Rabbit and the Tree Spirit
Lina Mao Wall
In this folktale from Cambodia, Judge Rabbit, a popular problem-solving creature who appears in many stories, is called upon to use his wits in the solution of a tricky problem facing a young couple. $14.95 **E**

Lion Dancer: Ernie Wan's Chinese New Year
Kate Waters
Ernie is about to dance in his first parade in New York's Chinatown. This is a photo-essay of his preparation and then the color and excitement of the New Year celebration. $4.99 **P, E**

Nine-in-One Grr! Grr!
Blia Xiong
This tale of how bird outsmarts the predator, tiger, is one the Hmong tell to explain the balance of nature. Illustrated in the style of Hmong embroidery. $6.95 **P, E**

The Dragon Lover and Other Chinese Proverbs
Yong-Sheng Xuan
Beautiful paper-cut illustrations accompany short tales, the morals of which are traditional Chinese proverbs. The stories are similar to traditional Western morality tales, but the illustrations are unique and wonderful. $15.95 **P, E**

Weighing the Elephant
Ting-xing Ye
In a village of southern China, a baby elephant has captured the hearts of the people, and especially a boy. When the greedy emperor hears about the intelligence of this particular elephant, he decrees that the elephant must be his. The parents of the baby ele-

phant and the young animal are separated, leading to great grief for the elephant parents and thus the villagers. When they appeal to the emperor, he gives them one way to reunite the family, and the young boy figures out, using displacement, how to weigh the elephant! Wonderful illustrations, and a good lesson about the ways both elephants and people care for one another. $5.95 **E**

Why Rat Comes First
Clara Yen
This is a story of the Chinese Zodiac explaining how the clever rat became the first animal in the Chinese calendar cycle of 12 years. $14.95 **P, E**

Books by
Laurence Yep Laurence Yep writes about Chinese Americans, helping us to understand the strong ties of Chinese culture and how the racism of many Americans have affected those who have come here from China to seek a new life.

The Amah
Amy Chin's mother has taken a new job, as an amah for Stephanie. Although Stephanie is 12, like Amy, she needs a lot of taking care of, and Amy has to miss dance class almost every night to stay home with her younger brothers and sister. To make matters worse, Amy's mother comes home every day talking about how wonderful Stephanie is, while she seems to have nothing but criticism for Amy. At first Amy is hurt and resentful, but when the two girls finally meet, she begins to understand more about both Stephanie and her mother. Amy is an intelligent, interesting main character; her struggle to understand her mother's more Chinese ways of showing love make for a compelling read. $15.99 **M**

Child of the Owl
Twelve-year-old Casey learns to value her Chinese heritage in this story of life in San Francisco's Chinatown during the mid-1960s. $4.95 **M**

Dragonwings

Eight-year-old Moonshadow emigrates from China to San Francisco to join his father, a laundry worker with dreams of building a flying machine. Yep gives an unforgettable account of the 1906 earthquake and the intense racism the Chinese faced during and after the disaster. Highly recommended. $5.95 **M**

Rainbow People

Here, Yep has gathered together tales from 1930's Oakland Chinatown. The stories help shed light on Chinese-American life; they are all interesting and entertaining. $4.99 **M**

The Star Fisher

When Joan Lee's family opens the first laundry in Clarksburg, West Virginia, many residents have never seen a Chinese person before. Some are openly racist, while others are just afraid to make contact with strangers. With the help of a wonderful landlady, the Lee family finds that there are plenty of friendly folk, as well as dirty clothes, in Clarksburg. $4.99 **M**

xxxx

P = preschool
E = early elementary
M = middle school
Y = young adult
AA = all ages

European and Russian Heritage

Sovietrek: A Journey by Bicycle Across Russia
Dan Buettner
In 1990 the author put together a small team of riders and rode
from Minnesota to New York, flew across the Atlantic and cycled
through Europe and the old Soviet Union all the way to the Pacific.
The book focuses on the time the bikers spent in Russia, including
Siberia. We see the sights as well as many of the people they met.
A great way to find out about bike tripping and about Russia.
$23.95 **E, M**

One Boy from Kosovo
Trish Marx
Photographer Cindy Karp and the author documented the time 12-
year-old Edi Fejzullahu and his family spent in the Stakovac 1
refugee camp in Macedonia, after being forced out of their home in
Kosovo. In addition to helping young people understand the situation in the former Yugoslavia, this book helps kids (and adults)
understand the experience of being uprooted from your home,
school, extended family, friends and material possessions. This
family is able to return home after their stay in the camp, but the
refugee experience is profound, whether temporary or permanent.
$15.95 **E, M**

Elinda Who Danced in the Sky: An Estonian Folktale
Lynn Moroney
Elinda lives in the sky, directs the birds in their migrations and is
beloved by all. When suitors come to call, she rejects them one by
one: the North Star, the Sun and the Moon all fail to win her heart.

She finally finds the right match in the Lord of the Northern Lights, but decides not to marry because she wants to make her own independent way in the celestial world. $4.95 **P, E**

ℬ Uncle Vova's Tree
𝒞 Patricia Polacco
This story, based on the author's own Christmas memories, is a young girl's account of her last Christmas with her beloved uncle Vladmir, called Vova by his nieces and nephews. The Russian Christmas traditions are lovingly described, and the last pages show the magical happenings at the next Christmas, when all the local animals carry on Uncle Vova's tradition of decorating a tree outside. $5.95 **E**

ℬ Supergrandpa
David M. Schwartz
When 66-year-old Gustav Hakansson decided to enter the longest Swedish bicycle race ever, his family ridiculed him and the race's judges rejected him. He rode anyway, pedaling over 1,500 miles all day and all night, and won the race! According to the author, Supergrandpa lived to be 102 and has become a popular folk hero in Sweden. A great story with excellent illustrations. $4.95 **P, E**

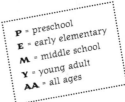

P = preschool
E = early elementary
M = middle school
Y = young adult
AA = all ages

Jewish-American and Holocaust Literature

A Picture Book of Anne Frank
David Adler
This book tells the story of Anne's life in hiding, why she was in danger and how she died. The illustrations of Anne and her family are taken from photographs; they enrich the simple text immeasurably. This is an excellent book for elementary students. $6.95 **E**

Tell Them We Remember: The Story of the Holocaust
Susan D. Bacharach
This book is a collection of stories, photographs and other information from the U.S. Holocaust Museum in Washington, D.C. Included is a chronology, information about resisters and enough information about the horrors of the Holocaust to make them real to kids. $12.95 **M**

Tell No One Who You Are
Walter Burchignani
Regine Miller was one of the children who went into hiding during the Nazi occupation of Europe, in this case in Belgium. Her story is one of great bravery; she was forced to cope with the loss of her loving family and deal with many cruel twists of fate before finding a place where she was cared for with any kindness at all. $8.95 **E**

Make a Wish, Molly
Barbara Cohen
Molly has been invited to a birthday party at the home of one of her non-Jewish friends from school. Her family has recently arrived from Russia, and the time is probably the early part of this century.

Molly's excitement turns to dread when her mother reminds her that the party is during Passover, and Molly cannot eat the leavened cake! Molly's creative mother comes to the rescue with a solution that helps Molly and her new friends come together. $5.50 **E**

Molly's Pilgrim
Barbara Cohen
Russian immigrant Molly and the rest of her class learn a valuable lesson about all the different kinds of pilgrims there are, with the help of a wise teacher and Molly's creative mother. $3.50 **E, M**

Thank You, Jackie Robinson
Barbara Cohen
Sam, a young Jewish boy, and Davy, an old, black, Christian man, couldn't be more different. But they both love the Brooklyn Dodgers, and they slowly develop a close friendship. When Davy gets sick, Sam wants to do something special for him. $4.95 **E, M**

Remember Not to Forget
Norman Finkelstein
A simple picture book documents the history of anti-Semitism for young people. The book ends by explaining the importance of keeping history alive so people will not allow such horrific events to happen again. $4.95 **E**

Letters from Rifka
Karen Hesse
Rifka and her family have taken the dangerous step of fleeing Russia for America, but Rifka may be stuck in Europe. When her family completes the difficult trip across the Continent, Rifka is not allowed to get on the boat because of a contagious disease she picked up on the route. Will she ever be able to join her family in America? A terrific, suspenseful read. $4.99 **M**

Sky: A True Story of Courage During World War II
Hanneke Ippisch
The author, beginning when she was 18, was part of the resistance to the Nazis in Holland. She courageously changed her identity and brought Jews across the border to safety. She managed to elude the Nazis for years until she was caught and thrown into prison. The story of her years in the Resistance and in prison is riveting, and she has many photos and actual documents she was able to save. $15.95 **Y**

Number the Stars
Lois Lowry
Ten-year-old Annemarie becomes part of the Danish Resistance to Nazi occupation when her family shelters her Jewish best friend Ellen and pretends she is part of the family. A real page-turner! $4.50 **M**

Alan and Naomi
Myron Levoy
The last thing Alan Silverman wants to do is give up playing stickball with the guys and spend his afternoons with a crazy French girl. But Alan slowly grows and learns from Naomi, whose experiences with the Nazis in France have closed her to the outside world. The portraits of these two young people in 1944's New York are accurate and fascinating. $4.95 **M**

The Lily Cupboard
Shulamith Levey Oppenheim
Set in the Netherlands during the Nazi occupation, this gentle picture book shows one child's experience of being sheltered by a brave Dutch family. Because it focuses on the kindness of people such as those taking care of Miriam, this is a good way to begin talking about the Holocaust with young children. $5.95 **E**

The Devil in Vienna
Doris Orgel
Inge and Liselotte are friends in 1937 Vienna. Inge is Jewish, while Liselotte's father is a Nazi. They secretly remain friends until Inge's family is forced to flee. $5.99   **M, Y**

Tikvah Means Hope
Patricia Polacco
Justine and Duane help their neighbors, Mr. and Mrs. Roth, build a sukkah so they can all sleep out under the stars. As always, Polacco brings together a mix of cultures, fostering growth for all concerned. $5.99   **P, E**

What Zeesie Saw on Delancey Street
Elsa Okon Real
In this Caldecott honor book, illustrated by Marjorie Priceman, it is Zeesie's seventh birthday. Her parents are bringing her to her first "package party," where immigrants already living in New York come together to auction off food they have made to raise money for new immigrants from Eastern Europe. $16.00   **P, E**

The Devil's Arithmetic
Jane Yolen
Hannah is bored sitting through yet another Passover Seder with her family, listening to their talk of the past. But this Passover is different; Hannah is transported to Poland during the Nazi occupation, where she comes face to face with the horrors of the Holocaust. $4.99   **M**

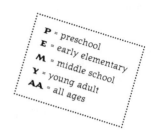

P = preschool
E = early elementary
M = middle school
Y = young adult
AA = all ages

The Middle East

Ramadan
Suhaib Hamid Ghazi
How many of us know the significance of Ramadan? This book follows Hakeem and his family during this holy month, when the family sits together for special meals before dawn and after dark, fasts all day, and goes to the mosque every night. The month is a time to end arguments, as well as to remember that the hunger one feels is hunger poor people feel always. The illustrations by Omar Rayyan are beautiful, stylized watercolors, using the themes of Arabic artwork, but also showing a contemporary American child. $6.95 **E**

The Day of Ahmed's Secret
Florence Parry Heide
Vibrant watercolors give us a feel for the daily bustle of life in Cairo, Egypt. Ahmed delivers fuel in his wagon pulled by a donkey, waiting all day to share his secret—that he has learned to write his name! $5.95 **P, E**

House of Wisdom
Florence Parry Heide and Judith Heide Gilliland
Baghdad has become, in U.S. political rhetoric, a city where dropping bombs was acceptable to most Americans. In A.D. 830, the Caliph of Baghdad supervised the building of the House of Learning, a library and one of the great centers of thought and new ideas in the world. This book is based on the life of its most famous

scholar, Ishaq, who dedicated his life to the translation of Aristotle. The story revolves around Ishaq's discovery, after travelling around the world in search of new books, ideas and experiences, of the excitement and wonders of a life of learning. $16.95 **E**

Kiss the Dust
Elizabeth Laird
Tara Hawrami is a 12-year-old Iraqi Kurd girl who lives happily with her family in a beautiful house in the city. In a compelling story, Laird weaves the history of the brutal treatment of the Kurds and their resistance together with the fictional account of Tara's family's forced migration from their home. They must travel into the mountains and eventually are exiled. A great book to help kids look beyond news headlines. $4.99 **M**

The Winged Cat
Deborah Nourse Lattimore
In this tale of Ancient Egypt, Merit is a young girl who serves in the temple of the cat goddess. When she sees an important priest killing a cat, her courage and integrity help her win a life-and-death struggle. The author recreates some of the art, beliefs and everyday life of the ancient world in this interesting tale. $5.95 **P, E, M**

Magid Fasts for Ramadan
Mary Matthews
Set in contemporary Egypt during Ramadan, the period when Muslims eat and drink only before sunrise and after sunset, this book focuses on seven-year-old Magid and his desire to be a good Muslim. Since his parents tell him he is too young to fast, he decides to fast in secret. He is found out, of course, and the resolution is positive for all. $6.95 **E**

Our Multicultural Society

P = preschool
E = early elementary
M = middle school
Y = young adult
AA = all ages

New Kids in Town: Oral Histories of Immigrant Teens

Jane Bode

These teenagers have mainly come from Asia and Latin America; they tell fascinating stories, variations of which are shared by more and more high-school students in the United States today.
$4.50   **M, Y**

Celebrations Series

This series of books looks at various celebrations, with color photographs and words, showing the way these holidays are celebrated at home and in a multicultural classroom in England. Each book includes a glossary and some suggested activities.   **E**

Diwali
Chris Deshpande
The Hindu Festival of Lights. $5.95

Sam's Passover
Lynne Hannigan
The Jewish feast and retelling of the Jews' exodus from Egypt. $5.95

Dat's New Year
Linda Smith
The Chinese New Year. $4.95

Eid-Ul-Fur
Susheila Stone
The Islamic celebration at the end of Ramadan. $4.95

Coming of Age in America:
A Multicultural Anthology
Mary Frosch, ed.
A collection featuring many important writers on the current scene,
including Julia Alvarez, Dorothy Allison and Frank Chin. $12.95
M, Y

Join In: Multiethnic Short Stories by Outstanding
Writers for Young Adults
Donald Gallo
Rudolfo Anaya, Sharon Bell Mathis, Linda Crew and Julius Lester are
among the authors whose work is included in this collection of
writing exploring such important subjects as friendship, prejudice,
fairness and confrontation. Many ethnic backgrounds are represented in this volume. $5.50   **Y**

What Are You? Voices of Mixed-Race Young People
Pearl Fuyo Gaskins
Young adults in their later teens and early twenties share stories,
poems and opinions about growing up biracial or multiracial in
America. They talk with humor, honesty and insight about such
issues as dating, hair, grandparents, racism, food and which box to
fill in when asked about their heritage. $18.95   **Y**

Come On, Rain!
Karen Hesse
Karen Hesse's poetry perfectly captures the feeling of a sweltering
day in Tess's neighborhood. When the rain finally comes, Tess and
her friends are so happy they go out and dance in it. At first their
mothers yell for them to come inside, but even the mothers cannot
resist celebrating the glorious rain. John J. Muth's watercolors are
unique and wonderful. $15.95   **P, E**

Journey Between Two Worlds Series

Each book features a family who has left a dangerous or repressive situation to make a new home in the United States. The photos and text inform the reader about both the early life and the current life of the family. There is also information about each country of origin. $8.95 **P, E**

Russian Jewish Family
Jane Nersky Leder

Guatemalan Family
Michael Malone

Kurdish Family
Karen O'Connor

The Colors of Us
Karen Katz
At first, the young narrator of this story thinks brown is brown, but as she explores her school and neighborhood, she realizes everyone is a different, beautiful hue. The illustrations are brightly colored, appealing collages. $15.95 **P, E**

All the Colors We Are/ Todos los Colores de Nuestra Piel
Katie Kissinger
In a colorful, photo-laden book, the author explains why we are the colors we are. In simple language, she explains how we are all colored by the amount of pigment we carry in our skin as well as our exposure to the sun. A good book to help open the discussion of skin color and what it means. Bilingual in Spanish and English. $9.95 **P, E**

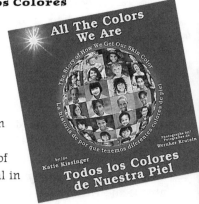

A Is for the Americas
Cynthia Chin Lee and Terri de la Peña
This excellent alphabet book celebrates geographical and cultural phenomena from all over the Americas. B is for Bison, C for Carnival and D for Dia de los Muertes (Day of the Dead); these and many more are explained in detail and accompanied by Enrique O. Sanchez's beautiful paintings. $15.95 **P, E**

Dave at Night
Gail Carson Levine
The author draws on her own father's experience as an orphan in a Jewish asylum during the Great Depression. The fictionalized Hebrew Home for Boys, or Hell Hole for Brats, as the boys call it, is in Harlem; Dave escapes one night into the world of the Harlem Renaissance, and his life is changed forever. From the poverty and cruelty of his life as an orphan to the rich musical and cultural atmosphere he falls in love with, Dave's experiences will surely captivate the reader. $15.95 **M**

Prejudice: A Story Collection
Edited by Daphne Muse
Muse has put together a terrific collection, which includes stories by Sandra Cisneros, Jacqueline Woodson and Flannery O'Connor, among many others. This book will inspire deep thought and discussion about what constitutes prejudice and what we can do to stop it. $7.95 **M, Y**

Chicken Sunday
Patricia Polacco
A Young Russian-American girl and her best friends, two African-American brothers, desperately want to buy the Easter hat the boys' grandmother has been admiring. But when they go into Mr. Kodinski's hat shop, he thinks they are the people who vandalized his store earlier. The kids decide to show Mr. Kodinski he is wrong about them by decorating some Pysanky eggs for him. Eventually, Mr. Kodinski realizes his mistake, and the kids are able to surprise Miss Eula with the hat she wants. $5.99 **P, E**

Mrs. Katz and Tush

Patricia Polacco

Mrs. Katz is an elderly, recently widowed, Jewish woman who befriends Larnel, a young African-American boy. Tush is the kitten who brings them together and helps them become family to each other, a relationship that lasts the rest of Mrs. Katz's life, including celebrating Jewish holidays together. $6.99 **P, E**

Just Like Me: Stories and Self-Portraits by 14 Artists

Edited by Harriet Rohmer

None of these talented women and men are household names; all are ethnic minorities in the U.S., and all are dedicated artists. Each discusses how he or she was drawn in childhood to art or to the visual world and how they came to the type of art they currently produce. All the self-portraits are very different and would interest and inspire a young artist. $15.95 **E, M**

Quilted Landscape: Conversations with Young Immigrants

Yale Strom

This book tells the stories of 26 young people, ages ten through 17, who have moved from countries all over the globe to different places in the United States. There is background information about each country, but the bulk of the text is each young person's story, told in the first person. $18.00 **P, E**

Yoko

Rosemary Wells

Yoko's mother sends her to school with a beautiful cooler of her favorite sushi. At lunch, the other children all tease her about eating raw fish and seaweed. The teacher helps ease this problem by having an international food day. Yoko is an outstandingly appealing green-eyed kitten, and other "children" are raccoons, bulldogs, pigs, all drawn in a colorful, clear and attractive style. $14.95 **P, E**

More, More, More Said the Baby: Three Love Stories
Vera B. Williams
In this simple, beautiful book for young children, three babies play
with the grownups who love them. Little Guy, Little Pumpkin and
Little Bird are all of different races, playing with different family
members, but all three are mischievous, adorable and well loved.
$4.95 **P**

Scooter

Vera B. Williams
Elana is a city child, daughter of a single mother, living in a building with families of every ethnic background. Her story is a positive look at the potential life of a working class child in New York,
with all the characters living in her neighborhood creating a fascinating backdrop for a growing child. Her pain at the neglect of her
father is present, but so is her joy at the many other aspects of her
life. $15.00 **M**

The Wonderful Towers of Watts

Patricia Zelver
Simon Rodia was an Italian immigrant who collected tile fragments,
of broken bottles, seashells and much more. Over the years, he
built extraordinary multicolored towers from this "garbage" that
still stand in the Watts neighborhood of Los Angeles. $4.95 **P, E**

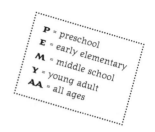

P = preschool
E = early elementary
M = middle school
Y = young adult
AA = all ages

Adoption

Zachary's New Home: A Story for Foster and Adopted Children

Geraldine Blomquist

Zachary is a small kitten. When his father leaves, his mother becomes abusive, and he is taken into a foster home. All the adults he encounters are very kind to him, and he is adopted by Tom and Marie, a couple of geese. His adjustment is rocky, but by the end he is getting settled and recovering. A good book to help kids discuss their feelings and experiences. $8.95 **P, E**

The Mulberry Bird

Anne Braff Brodzinsky

Mother bird is a young songbird, anxiously preparing for her first baby to hatch. She has no partner and no support from other birds. When she becomes overwhelmed with the responsibilities of caring for her baby, she visits the owl, who advises her to come with him to find a family of birds who will love and care for her baby. At first she resists the idea, but a bad storm shows her that she can't protect her baby. She and the owl find a family of shore birds with a warm, empty nest waiting for a baby to fill it. Mother bird is sad, but knows she has done the right thing for her baby. $16.00 **E**

Abby

Jeanette Caines

After hurting Abby's feelings by refusing to read her the book containing the story of her adoption, Abby's older brother Kevin shows how much he really does love her. $5.95 **P, E**

Tell Me Again About the Night I Was Born
Jamie Lee Curtis

Lively and funny pictures accompany the text of this book in which
every page begins with "tell me again about...." The parents receive
a phone call, telling them to get on a plane and pick up their new
daughter at the hospital. The daughter wants to hear again about
"how tiny and perfect I was" and about the first night "you were my
daddy and you told me about baseball being the perfect game, just
like your daddy told you." $16.95 **P, E**

Adoption Is for Always
Linda Walvoord Girard

Celia was adopted as an infant. Although her parents have always
been open with her, when she reaches the age where the fact
of her adoption is meaningful, she needs lots of assurance that she
belongs with her parents forever. $5.95 **E**

We Adopted You, Benjamin Koo
Linda Walvoord Girard

In this book, nine-year-old Benjamin Koo Andrews tells about his
life and feelings as a Korean boy adopted as an infant into a white
family in the United States. He is clearly in a loving, culturally
aware family, and he is able to be very perceptive and honest
about the hard times as well as the good times in his life so far.
$6.95 **E, M**

A Mother for Choco
Keiko Kasza

Choco is a small bird who wishes he had a
mother. He asks all the different animals he
encounters if each could be his mother. Each
has her own reason not to care for Choco,
until he finds Mrs. Bear, who already has a
brood of very different but much loved children and can't wait for Choco to be part of

the family. A charming revision of the "Are You My Mother?"
matching story and a good way to start talking with young children about interracial or intercultural adoption. $5.95 **P**

Over the Moon
Karen Katz
This is one of our favorite adoption books; the story of this baby's
arrival from Central America, while romanticized, follows the basic
story of many of us who have adopted from abroad. The telephone
call lets us know we can pack and fly on the next airplane to meet
our new child. The artwork and story are filled with joy, flowers,
color and love. What a wonderful way for adopted children to feel
they were truly welcomed into this world! $15.95 **P, E**

Horace
Holly Keller
Horace's parents are tigers, and he is a young leopard. Every night
his mother tells him the story about how she and his father chose
him because he had lost his family when he was a baby, and they
liked his spots and wanted him to be their child. One day, Horace
decides to find his real family. He finds a leopard family and plays
with them all day, but when the day ends, he is glad to be home
where he knows he belongs. $4.95 **P, E**

Tall Boy's Journey
Joanna Halpert Kraus
The author adopted her son from Korea when he was eight-and-
a-half years old. In this book , she draws on his experiences as
well as the experiences of other Korean children adopted by
American parents. When Kim Moo Yong's grandmother dies, he
has no remaining relatives who can care for him, and he must
come to America. The author does a fantastic job of showing us
how this country appears to a frightened Korean boy. $19.95 **E**

How It Feels to Be Adopted

Jill Krementz

Nineteen boys and girls, ages eight to 16, discuss their feelings about being adopted, how they feel about finding or not finding their birth parents, and the role being adopted plays in their lives. A great resource for kids and parents, this book shows the variety of feelings and experiences that come with being an adopted child. $15.00 **M, Y**

Happy Adoption Day!

John McCutcheon

The words to McCutcheon's original song "Happy Adoption Day" are illustrated with a delightful, colorful, picture-story tale of a mother and father preparing the bedroom, taking off on a plane, probably to Asia, and coming back with a baby who soon grows into a toddler. The Adoption Day party has all the essentials: cake, grandma, friends, pets and good cheer. $15.95 **P, E**

Pablo's Tree

Pat Mora

A lovely story about a small boy's fifth birthday and the special tradition he has with his grandfather, Lito. When Pablo's mother decided to adopt a baby, Lito got a tree for his new grandson. He did not plant the tree until after he held Pablo in his arms for the first time. Ever since, he has decorated the tree in a special way every year on Pablo's birthday. $16.00 **P, E**

Twice Upon a Time

Eleanore Patterson

A story about being born and adopted, with good information about both events. Mainly deals with adoption by married couples. $5.99 **P, E**

Mommy Far, Mommy Near
Carol Antoinette Peacock

This book helps deal with the concept of a birth mother living far away, with whom a connection is not possible. In this case, the daughter questions her mother about her other mother in China, and why she might not have been able to keep Elizabeth. Her mother explains that her birth mother acted out of love and because she had no choice in her situation, giving a simple explanation of China's one-child policy. $14.95 E

Through Moon and Stars and Night Skies
Ann Turner

A view of adoption through the eyes of an Asian child, about five years old, who is adopted by parents in the United States. He tells of his trip on the plane and his first encounters with his parents and his new home. A very simple and touching story. $5.95 P, E

Real Sisters
Susan Wright

Claire's brown skin makes her look very different from her light-skinned older sister Jenny. When she enters a new school, some of the kids tease her, saying that she and Jenny aren't real sisters. A realistic and reassuring look at kids' experiences with interracial adoption, and what makes people real members of the same family. $5.95 E

P = preschool
E = early elementary
M = middle school
Y = young adult
AA = all ages

Family Diversity

The Families Book: True Stories About Real Kids and the People They Live With
Arlene Erlbach

In the first part of the book, 35 kids from eight to 18 talk about their families, whether they live in blended families, a group home, have parents of different races or the same gender, have lots of siblings or have adopted siblings. All the kids featured have loving, supportive home lives. The second section of the book is activities for kids to help them understand their own family's history and unique attributes. This is a great resource for kids who are exploring who they are and want to go into a bit more depth than basic conversation. $12.95 **E, M**

Love Makes a Family:
Portraits of Lesbian, Gay, Bisexual and Transgender Parents and Their Families
Edited by Peggy Gillespie

In beautiful black and white portraits, photographer Gigi Kaeser has captured the love that is abundant in all these families. Peggy Gillespie has collected stories from both children and adults about what it is like to live in a nontraditional family. Many of the families are also racially blended; the photos will stretch kids' ideas about what constitutes a family, while the words will interest and inspire adults. $19.95 **M, Y**

Celebrating Families
Rosemarie Hausherr

In a beautiful format, this book looks at family diversity, with portraits of a child's family, and also a photo of a typical family activity. The text describes the basic way in which each family is unique. This book's families are all colors, economic backgrounds, and include foster families, a homeless family, co-housing, adoption by a lesbian couple, extended family and more. An excellent tool to help kids understand that each family is one of the typical American families of the late 20th century. $16.95 **P, E**

Families: A Celebration of Diversity, Commitment and Love
Aylette Jenness
How do you define a family? Step, extended, gay, lesbian, foster, divorced, adoptive, communal and religious families are all represented in this book of photos and text by each of 17 kids. $5.95 **AA**

Welcoming Babies
Margy Burns Knight
A lovely book describing some of the many rituals around the world used for welcoming babies. Each page describes a different baby and is headed with "We sing, we promise, we announce," etc. The artwork is very attractive. $7.95 **P, E**

My Mother's Getting Married
Joan Krescher
Katy is filled with mixed feelings about her mother's upcoming marriage, even though she clearly likes her stepfather. Terrific illustrations and Katie's spunky personality make this story a fun read. $3.95 **E**

Do I Have a Daddy? A Story About a Single-Parent Child
Jeanne Warren Lindsay
A simple story about a single mother and how she handles her son's questions about his father, who has never been involved in his care. A section at the end is addressed to single mothers. $6.95 **P, E**

Families

Ann Morris

This book is actually part of a series listed ahead, but it's important to highlight this new offering into the field of books showing the many different forms families can take. The families in this book are many different ethnicities, combinations of extended family members, large and small families, and adoptive, step and one clearly lesbian family. The photos are terrific; the text is simple enough for the youngest child; and there is a description of the location and what's happening in most of the pictures at the end of the book. $15.95 **P, E**

Families Are Different

Nina Pellegrini

Nico, the young narrator, is an adopted Korean kid. In this very simple book, she describes her family and her feelings about being adopted into a family with parents who don't look like her, and then she briefly describes some other families she knows. $16.95 **P, E**

Who's in a Family?

Robert Skutch

This is one of the better books with the positive message that families are whoever you live with and love. $6.95 **P, E**

Families

Meredith Tax

Feminist Press has reissued this book, and the illustrations have been colored with pastels, giving it a new look. The text remains the same, though, and the message, "Families are who you live with and who you love" can never be heard too many times. Lots of varied families, and the new illustrations are bright and fun. Also available in Spanish. $7.95 **P, E**

P = preschool
E = early elementary
M = middle school
Y = young adult
AA = all ages

People Around the World

Children from Australia to Zimbabwe:
A Photographic Journey Around the World
Maya Ajmera and Anna Rhesa Versola
Lives of children from countries in every part of the world are
described here, as well as pictured. This is a book that is tempting
to pick up and leaf through, stopping at the country that might
interest the reader, where he or she can learn about schools, the
climate, the food and even the names of other countries beginning
with the same letter! $18.95 **E, M**

A Ride on Mother's Back: A Day of Baby Carrying
Around the World
Emery and Durga Bernhard
Babies all around the world ride on their mothers' backs, but in
each place they are carried a little differently, and to very different
places. In a book with lovely artwork and a concept sure to please
young children, babies from Papua New Guinea, Canada's far
north, West Africa, the Andes mountains and more locations share
their parents' days from the back or hip of a loved one. $6.00 **P, E**

Birthdays: Celebrating Life Around the World
Eve B. Feldman
Artwork by children, collected by the organization "Paintbrush
Diplomacy," shows the many different birthday customs in countries in every region of the world. The verse describing the birthday customs is simple, and the pictures are wonderful. After the
main text, there is more information about how birthdays are celebrated in each of the countries portrayed. $14.95 **P, E**

A Calendar of Festivals
Cherry Gilchrist

Eight different holidays from different cultures and religions are first introduced, then explained; each holiday's defining story or legend is told here. The festivals include Vesak, which celebrates the start of Buddha's wisdom teachings, and Purim, the Jewish holiday celebrating the biblical Esther. The illustrations are beautiful, as are the illustrations in all the books from this English publisher, Barefoot Books. $18.95 **E**

In the Beginning: Creation Stories from Around the World
Virginia Hamilton

This book contains 25 creation stories from all over the world. The selection shows both the diversity of ideas about creation and the themes that are shared by many cultures. $15.00 **AA**

Wake Up, World: A Day in the Life of Children Around the World
Beatrice Hollyer

A beautiful photo book highlights eight children and the way they spend their days. Find out how Cidinha from Brazil, Linh from Vietnam, Sasha from Russia and the others sleep, eat, learn, play and do chores on a typical day. $16.95 **P, E**

Two Eyes, a Nose and a Mouth
Roberta Grobel Intrater

This book for young children has one theme: the differences in our faces are relatively minor, and the world is a much more interesting and wonderful place because we are all different. There are many full-page illustrations of different people's faces, but the two-page spreads of many faces, one containing all different faces representing all different ages and ethnic groups, and the other spread with hundreds of pictures of the same face, eloquently show kids how much better it is to have a world full of different folks. $5.99 **P**

Children Just Like Me

Barnabas and Anabel Kindersley in
association with UNICEF

More than 30 children from every
populated continent are photographed and interviewed about their
lives and dreams for the future.
Information about each of the countries from which children have been
chosen is presented in an exciting
and inviting format. This book takes
us to every region of the world, with
written and visual information about
food, housing, school, fun and family
in each place. Find out what Aseye
from Ghana likes to eat, what games Edgar from the Philippines
likes to play, what kind of pet lives with Monika from Budapest,
and much, much more! $6.95, $16.95 CLOTH **AA**

Children Just Like Me: Celebrations

Barnabas and Anabel Kindersley

From Hina Matsuri (a Japanese holiday dedicated to dolls), to
Fassika (the Ethiopian Easter), to the ways in which many cultures
celebrate the changing of the seasons, this beautiful book is full
of colorful photographs and information about how children
around the world mark the passing of each year. $17.95 **P, E, M**

Children Just Like Me: Our Favorite Stories

Jamila Gavin

Some of the children from the original book, *Children Just Like Me*,
are back with one story each from their countries. The illustrations
are wonderful paintings by artist Amanda Hall, and the stories are
enhanced with sidebars with cultural artifacts and information,
and natural history that helps the reader appreciate the background of the story. $14.95 **E, M**

Market
Ted Lewin
The open-air market is found in all parts of the world. People go to
market on foot or by mule, truck or bicycle, and bring things they
grow, make or catch, but regardless of these differences, all markets are places people gather to buy, sell and socialize. Lewin's
marvelous, lively paintings and text describe markets in the Andes,
New York City, Nepal and Uganda, among other widely diverse
locations. $6.95 **P, E**

The Barefoot Book of Tropical Tales
Raouf Mama
This Beninese storyteller has collected eight tales from Benin, Haiti,
Sri Lanka, Antigua, Puerto Rico, the Cape Verde Islands, Malaysia
and Zimbabwe. All of these stories have a moral—respect your
elders; the benefits of hard work, loyalty and kindness; and the
problems from greed, envy, lying and cruelty. The illustrations
by Dierdre Hyde are colorful and striking, with attractive borders
around each page, making every page a work of art. $19.95 **AA**

Photograph Books by Ann Morris and Ken Heyman
Each book in this popular series for young children is built around
a theme (see titles of individual books) and is full of photos from
around the world. The photos show the many variations around
the world on universally recognized objects, ceremonies and ideas,
and many of the photos are of children. The text is very simple,
and at the end of the book there is an explanation of each location
and some information for adults and older children about each
photo. some of the books are available in paperback for $4.95;
HARDCOVERS ARE $15.00 **P, E**

> **Bread, Bread, Bread**
> **Families**
> **Hats, Hats, Hats**
> **Houses and Homes**
> **Loving**

On the Go
Play
Shoes, Shoes, Shoes
Weddings
Work

Vanishing Cultures Series

Jan Reynolds

Reynolds has lived among people of these traditional cultures, all of which are threatened by the encroachment of the modern world. She is committed to recording their ways of life before they are no longer in existence. Her photos, of kids, their families and their land, are fascinating, as is the accompanying text. $8.95 EACH. **E**

Amazon Basin

Tuwenowa, a Yanomamo boy, and his family live deep in the rainforest of Brazil, surviving entirely on what they glean from the forest. The photos and text bring new urgency to the efforts to save these people's ancient home.

Down Under

Reynolds lived with a group of Tiwi people off the northern coast of Australia in order to record their unique way of life. She photographs and writes about the ways in which they find food and shelter as well as the Tiwi concept of "the dreaming" and the importance of dance in Tiwi culture.

Far North

This is a portrait of a Sami family from Finmark, or Lapland. The Samis live above the Arctic Circle and depend on the reindeer for their food, clothing, transportation and livelihood.

Frozen North

Kenalogak is a young Inuit girl living on the Hudson Bay. She is finally old enough to begin learning to fish with her mother. She and her family live in the traditional Inuit way of life, a way of life that is now being threatened by increased hunting of caribou for sport.

Himalaya

Reynolds follows a young Sherpa girl and her family in Tibet. The photos of the people and the dramatic landscape are almost a trip to Tibet, minus the cold and altitude sickness.

Mongolia

The vast country of Mongolia is still largely undeveloped, and much of the population is made up of nomadic herders with close ties to their animals and the land on which they depend. Their lives are difficult; they must make efficient use of all their resources to survive in their barren but beautiful land. We see Mongolia through the eyes of Dawa and Olana, two boys who are receiving their first horses.

Sahara

The Tuareg people are nomads who live in the center of the huge Sahara desert. Manda, his whole family and all their possessions travel around the desert on the one camel they own.

Nine O'Clock Lullaby

Marilyn Singer

In this short trip around the world, Frané Lessac's delightful illustrations show us what is happening in many locations at the same time as bed-

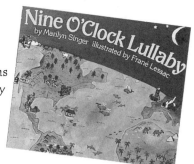

time in Brooklyn. Read about a party in Puerto Rico, fish and whales in the mid-Atlantic, dreaming children in Zaire, bicycle rush hour in China and much, much more. $5.95 **P, E**

Small World Series
Gwenyth Swain

These beautiful photograph books show children from all over the world taking part in everyday activities alone, with parents or with friends. The theme of this series is "things that bring us together." Young children will appreciate the engaging photos, the diversity of the children and settings, and the rhythmic, simple writing style. These are highly recommended. $5.95 **P, E**

Carrying
Celebrating
Eating
Smiling

P = preschool
E = early elementary
M = middle school
Y = young adult
AA = all ages

Gay and Lesbian Books

Free Your Mind: The Book for Gay, Lesbian and Bisexual Youth and Their Families
Ellen Bass and Kate Kaufman
This comprehensive book includes stories and quotes from famous gay and bisexual people, as well as advice from ordinary teenagers and young adults about the many aspects of being gay. Includes sections on everything from how to deal with friends and parents, to where to meet people, to activities. $14.00 **Y**

Am I Blue? Coming Out from the Silence
Marion Dane Bauer
This is a high-quality, low-cost collection of stories by terrific young adult authors, including Jacqueline Woodson, M. E. Kerr, Jane Yolen, William Sleator, Lois Lowry and many more. This book is highly recommended for all teens. $5.95 **Y**

Asha's Mums
Rosamund Elwin and Michele Paulse
At school, Asha's teacher questions her about the two mums on a form for a class trip. Sara and Alice come to school and help enlighten the class. A good introduction to a multiracial, loving, lesbian family. $5.95 **P, E**

OutSpoken: Role Models from the Lesbian and Gay Community
Michael Thomas Ford
In this excellent young adult book, Ford interviews a cartoonist, a writer, a teacher, an actor and a police officer, among others, all of whom publicly identify themselves as part of the gay community.

The interviewees discuss everything from how they knew they were gay, to how and when they came out, to where the gay community is headed and how young people can speak out for themselves and others. $4.95 Y

Reflections of a Rock Lobster
Aaron Fricke
The famous coming-out story of a young man who made national news by bringing a male date to his Rhode Island high-school prom. The book dates from 1981, but the issues haven't changed much and it is still an excellent book to give to teachers, as well as young people who are exploring their sexual identities. $5.95 Y

Annie on My Mind
Nancy Garden
Excellent coming out novel for young women, presenting both the joys and problems faced by two New York City high-school students. $4.95 Y

How Would You Feel If Your Dad Was Gay?
Ann Heron and Meredith Maran
Jasmine, Michael and Noah all have gay or lesbian parents—this story explores what happens when Jasmine tells her class that her dad is gay. When the kids and some teachers respond with ignorance and homophobia, the school has a program about families. A good discussion of whether kids want to be open or private about their parents' lifestyles. $6.95 E

Two Teenagers in Twenty: Writing by Gay and Lesbian Youth
Ann Heron
Ten years after the publication of *One Teenager in Ten*, Heron decided to collect writings by this newest generation of lesbian and gay youth. She has included some of the writings from the first collection and added the voices of teens from the '90s. This is an excel-

excellent book for gay and lesbian teens that will show them how many of their peers share similar feelings, questions and experiences. $10.95 **Y**

Night Kites
M. E. Kerr

Eric is a straight teen whose wonderful older brother is gay and has what is now known to be AIDS. A sensitive and compassionate novel by a popular author for teens, and one of the earliest young adult novels to deal with AIDS issues. $4.95 **Y**

The Shared Heart: Portraits and Stories Celebrating Lesbian, Gay and Bisexual Young People
Adam Mastoon

This book features beautiful photographs of and stories by young people from all different backgrounds; most of them have emerged from incredibly difficult adolescent years with remarkable courage and insight. Parents as well as teenagers of all sexual orientations will enjoy and learn from this exceptional book. $25.00 **Y**

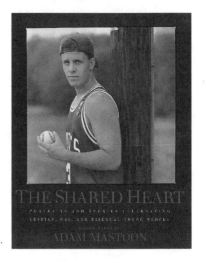

Heather Has Two Mommies
Leslea Newman

When Heather discovers that having two moms is "different," she also discovers that "the most important thing in a family is that everyone in it loves each other." $8.95 **P, E**

Young, Gay and Proud, Fourth Edition
Dan Romesburg
Short but clear chapters deal with every issue from who and how to tell about your sexuality, to health, how to meet people, stereotypes and how to fight them, to book and film resources. $5.95 Y

Growing Up Gay: A Literary Anthology
Bennett Singer, ed.
This collection will be a lifeline for lesbian and gay teens, many of whom still feel isolated in small towns and conservative cities and suburbs. The pieces are all fairly short, with writing by many of the best known lesbian and gay authors, from many different backgrounds. $9.95 Y

Hearing Us Out: Voices from the Lesbian and Gay Community
Roger Sutton
This book includes the life stories of a number of people with all sorts of roles in the gay community, from AIDS activists to lesbian moms to a drag queen. A reassuring and useful book for teens who want to understand what being gay is about. $16.95 Y

Daddy's Roommate
Michael Willhoite
A young boy thoroughly enjoys the weekend with his divorced father and his father's lover. The middle-class setting is a bit squeaky clean, but it's a fun book to read and the pictures are colorful and lively. $9.95 P, E

P = preschool
E = early elementary
M = middle school
Y = young adult
AA = all ages

War and Peace, Justice and Righteous Acts

Strike

Maureen Bayless

Molly's mother is on strike at the cannery, and neither Molly nor her mother is happy about it. When Molly is down at the plant with her mother, her quick thinking and thoughtful message to some truckers outside the cannery help to end the strike.
$5.95 **P, E**

Charlie Pippin

Candy Dawson Boyd

Charlie is an independent girl who refuses to put aside her questions about the Vietnam War and her father's devastating experiences there. Her involvement in politics and the way she confronts both her father and history make memorable reading.
$4.99 **M, Y**

Sweet Dried Apples:
A Vietnamese Wartime Childhood

Rosemary Breckler

Lieu's peaceful childhood in rural Vietnam is first interrupted when her father leaves to join the army and her grandfather comes to live with the family. He is a revered and wise herbal healer, and Lieu and her brother learn many things working with him. The bigger interruption comes when war destroys their village and they are forced to flee. Inspired by the experiences of a friend of the author. $15.95 **E**

So Far from the Sea

Eve Bunting

Many contemporary Japanese-American families have memories of the bleak period of internment during World War Two. For this family, the visit to Manzanar to honor the grave of the grandfather who died there is a profound and sad experience. The paintings show the contemporary, bleak, cold setting, surrounded by high peaks, and tell about the life of the prison camp half a century ago. We understand to a small degree how it might have been for these sea-loving people to be imprisoned in this bleak and strange place. $15.00 **E**

Meiko and the Fifth Treasure

Eleanor Coerr

This book tells Meiko's story of surviving the Nagasaki bombing, only to be sent to live with grandparents she barely knows while her parents remain behind to help the wounded. Her hand and her spirit are injured, and calligraphy has become impossible for her. With time, a supportive friend and her inner strength, she begins the process of recovery. $3.50 **E, M**

Sadako

Eleanor Coerr

The author of *Sadako and the Thousand Paper Cranes* and illustrator Ed Young have created a new picture book of Sadako's story. The pastels and the text blend together in a moving cry for world peace. $17.99 **E**

Sadako and the Thousand Paper Cranes

Eleanor Coerr

When she is hospitalized for leukemia, Sadako learns of a legend that if she can fold a thousand paper cranes, the gods will make her well. Sadako's classmates must complete the cranes for her, but the paper cranes have become a symbol of peace around the world. Sadako's courage, desire for peace and faith in the future in the face of the "atom bomb sickness," a result of the bombing of Hiroshima, have made her story world famous. $3.99 **E**

Big Book for Peace
Edited by Ann Durell
Over 30 well-known children's authors have contributed to this
anthology of stories, poems and pictures about peace. Among
the contributors are renowned authors Jean Craighead George,
Lois Lowry, Katherine Paterson, Yoshiko Uchida and Mildred Pitts
Walter. Illustrators include Maurice Sendak, Barbara Cooney,
Steven Kellogg, and Leo and Diane Dillon. $17.50 **E**

Song of the Buffalo Boy
Sherry Garland
Seventeen-year-old Loi is an Amerasian living in Vietnam. She
has always been shunned by most of the villagers because of her
American looks, but her boyfriend Khai has always stood by
her. When Loi is promised to a brutal military officer in marriage,
she runs away to Ho Chi Minh City, thinking she will emigrate to
the United States under the Refugee Resettlement Program. The
tremendous hardships she meets with in the city are countered by
her strength and the kindness she gives and receives. Her choice
to remain in Vietnam is a moving and thoughtful end to a
powerful book. $6.00 **Y**

This Land Is Your Land
Woody Guthrie, paintings by Kathy Jakobsen
Look again and again at the detailed, beautiful, folk-art-style paintings in this book, illustrating Woody Guthrie's classic folk song.
The artwork illustrates Guthrie's life, some of the most spectacular
natural wonders in the country, the contrast between the riches
of some and the poverty of others, and some scenes of how life
should be. $15.95 **AA**

The Journey: Japanese Americans, Racism
and Renewal
Sheila Hamanaka
The author is an artist who has created a five-panel mural docu-
menting the experience of Japanese Americans in the first half of

this century, but focusing on the internment camps. She looks at the camps in light of the racism and intolerance of those times, but she also makes it clear how closely we must guard against similar events happening, especially with the recent resurgence of anti-immigrant groups and laws. $8.95 **M, Y**

Barefoot Book of Heroic Children

Rebecca Hazell

Varied as the children in this beautiful book are, each influenced history at a young age, many overcoming great obstacles or surviving under circumstances many of us would find impossible. The author provides an introduction to the historical time and place of each of the children in the book, then each tells his or her "own story," and at the end the author again relates how that child's life continued (or did not). Included in the book are Sadako, Iqbal Masih (the Pakistani boy fighter against child labor), Anne Frank, Milarepa (one of the great teachers of Tibetan Buddhism), Fannie Mendelssohn and many others. The illustrations are the exceptional watercolors of illustrator Helen Cann. $19.95 **M**

Sami and the Time of the Troubles

Florence Parry Heide and Judith Heide Gilliland

This powerful work gives us a child's eye view of Beirut in wartime, a city that has become a symbol of endless conflict and killing. Illustrated with Ted Lewin's watercolors, this book makes us feel with Sami and his family the fear and frustration of having lives completely disrupted and losing family members to random and senseless killing. $6.95 **E, M**

A Time of Angels

Karen Hesse

A little-known epidemic of influenza in 1918 took the lives of 22 million people throughout the world. World War One was drawing to a close, which enabled many both then and now to ignore the epidemic. Hannah's life is changed drastically by both events. She is separated from her family, and when the flu hits her close-knit Boston tenement neighborhood, she leaves for her safety, fleeing to Vermont. Hannah gets sick anyway, and while recovering, she is taken in by an elderly German-American man. She learns many lessons from him—he is a strongly principled man who opposed the war. His kindness helps Hannah recover in many ways in this complex and rewarding story. $5.95 **M**

The Clay Marble
Mingfong Ho
In 1980, 12-year-old Dara and her remaining family make their way to the Thai border from their home in Cambodia to find the rumored food and farming supplies. Dara's experiences are both horrifying and strengthening for her, and we see how destructive the forces of war have been to the fabric of peasant life in Cambodia. Dara learns how to speak up for peace and for life-affirming activities in the face of war. $4.95 **M**

Long Time Passing
Adrienne Jones
A moving novel that perfectly captures the feeling of being young during the Vietnam war, and explores the conflicts and similarities of young people whose sympathies lay on both sides of the issue. Jonas has been raised on Marine bases; Auleen in a small town in Northern California. Auleen and her friends are passionately involved in the peace movement, while Jonas is torn. This is a fascinating novel, sure to help today's young people understand the issues facing their contemporaries 30 years ago. $15.95 **Y**

The Road from Home
David Kherdian
Kherdian's mother's experiences are the source for this extraordinary account of an Armenian girl's life during the Turkish genocidal war against the Armenians. The main character, Veron, the details of her bravery and the descriptions of Armenian culture and family life are so interesting that the book is hard to put down.
$4.95 **M, Y**

Onion Tears
Diana Kidd
Nam-Huong suffered the worst horrors of separation and loss of her family due to war in Vietnam. Flashbacks from the war are interspersed with her current life in Australia with her Vietnamese guardian, an older boy who is also a refugee and a spunky, caring teacher. $4.95 **M**

Talking Walls
Margy Bums Knight
Knight tells the stories of many cultures through the walls that are central to their worship, history and/or geology. The walls vary, from the Vietnam War monument in Washington, D.C., to Nelson Mandela's (former) prison walls, to the Great Wall of China and many lesser-known walls. Ann Sibley O'Brien's illustrations of people all over the world are truly amazing. $8.95 **E, M, Y**

Talking Walls: The Stories Continue
Margy Burns Knight
Expanding on the theme of their first book, Knight and O'Brien continue to portray walls of significance to many cultures around the world, including the Peace Wall in Russia and the Friendship Wall in Maine, lines separating neighborhoods in Belfast, Northern Ireland, and the Message Wall outside Pablo Neruda's home in Chile. $8.95 **E, M, Y**

Kids with Courage: True Stories About Young People Making a Difference
Barbara A. Lewis
The kids in this book have all made decisions to act in brave, unconventional ways. Reading these stories might motivate some kids to do the same. Some of these kids have spoken out in public against gangs or for the environment, while others have acted with generosity. $10.95 **E, M**

Kid's Guide to Social Action
Barbara A. Lewis

In this unique guide, kids can read stories of successful activism by young people, get addresses for organizations, learn how to identify the problem they want to deal with, and learn the nuts and bolts of lobbying, creating petition and letter drives, picketing, etc. Fairly mainstream in orientation, but a good start for kids who want to feel empowered and need a push into the world. $14.95 **E, M**

Baseball Saved Us
Ken Mochizuki

This book tells a young boy's story of his internment in a prison camp during World War Two. The prisoners were able to bear their humiliation and hardships with a new dignity when they created a baseball field with their own hands. The reader need not be a baseball fan to be moved by this book. $6.95 **E**

Habibi
Naomi Shihab Nye

At 14, Liyanna Abboud is not excited about leaving St. Louis to move to Jerusalem, near where her Palestinian father grew up. She is a thoughtful and observant girl, and there is much to learn in this land of frequent violence and conflict, as well as fascinating history and great beauty. She becomes friendly with two children living in a Palestinian refugee camp, and begins a close relationship with a sensitive Jewish boy. She meets her hundreds of Palestinian relatives, and especially gets close with her Sitti, her grandmother. This rich novel expresses the hope for future peace when Palestinians and Israelis can live together, creating a new kind of life. $4.99 **M**

A Time to Fight Back: True Stories of Wartime Resistance

Jayne Pettit

The author has focused on eight young people who were caught in the horrors and injustice of World War Two; each found his or her own path to resist oppression or help save lives. A moving account of the abilities of young people when they are faced with a life-or-death situation. This book should help provoke thoughts about how those of us living a comfortable life might act in the face of a crisis. $14.95 **M**

Pink and Say

Patricia Polacco

When two young Union soldiers in the Civil War attempt to rejoin their unit, they are captured and sent to the notorious prison camp, Andersonville. The friendship endures the tragic death of one of the boys, with a sad ending sure to bring tears to any reader. $15.99 **E**

Shades of Gray

Carolyn Reeder

At the end of the Civil War, Will's immediate family is dead, and he must live with his aunt and uncle, who are much poorer than his family was and live on a farm. Will's father died fighting for the Confederacy, but his uncle refused to serve in the army. Will's anger at his uncle turns into grudging respect and then love as he learns there are different sorts of bravery. $4.99 **M**

After the Dancing Days

Margaret Rostkowski

World War One has ended for most Americans, but Annie has lost her favorite uncle, and becomes friendly with a severely wounded veteran. As Annie helps Andrew regain his life, she learns to question conventional ideas of patriotism and heroism. This beautifully written book effectively challenges the beliefs that allow wars to exist. Highly recommended. $4.95 **M, Y**

Peace Begins with You
Katherine Scholes

An idea whose time has come This book explores peace in global and personal ways, clearly linking justice with peace-"peace is having all the things you need." This book is a great beginning for thinking or discussion and, we hope, a push for kids to become peacemakers. $7.95 **E**

Listen to Us: The World's Working Children
Jane Springer

In a world where children are forced to labor, often all their waking hours, this important book both describes the problem in a variety of countries and documents what young people in both the developed and developing world are doing to try to solve this horrendous problem. This is an important book with great information, as well as a spur to activism. $16.95 **M, Y**

I Am an American: The True Story of
Japanese Internment
Jerry Stanley

A true story of one Japanese-American family's encounter with the terrible injustice of the United States' policy of jailing Japanese Americans during World War Two. $15.95 **E, M**

People Power: A Look at Nonviolent
Action and Defense
Susan Nieburg Terkel

The author covers much of the ground of the movement to nonviolently resist militarism, Greenpeace's actions, the Civil Rights movement, as well as older movements, such as resistance to the Third Reich in Germany and Ghandi's original pacifist revolution in India. The pictures are wonderful, recalling such events as the Deaf President Now protest at Gallaudet University and Clamshell Alliance protests. The result is a good overview, much of which will be unfamiliar to most young people. $17.99 **M**

The Three Little Wolves and the Big Bad Pig
Eugene Trivizas
In a wonderful reversal of the usual story that so fascinates kids, the little wolves use fortress-like construction materials to keep out the bad pig. Only when they decide to build their house with flowers do they charm the pig into friendship, and they all become companions. Great illustrations by Helen Oxenbury. $5.99 **P, E**

The Bracelet
Yoshiko Uchida
In 1942, Emi and her family are sent with other Japanese Americans to one of the bleak internment camps set up by the U.S. government. Before leaving. she is given a bracelet by her best friend to remember their friendship while she is away. $5.95 **E**

Stand Up for Your Rights
World Book Encyclopedia
Children from all over the world have contributed to this book celebrating the 50-year anniversary of the International Declaration of Human Rights. Along with their drawings and poems is information about what human rights are and how they have been won and taken away throughout history. $9.95 **E, M**

P = preschool
E = early elementary
M = middle school
Y = young adult
AA = all ages

Dealing with Violence and Injustice

Hear These Voices: Youth at the Edge of the Millenium

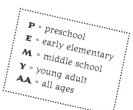

Anthony Allison

Allison has photographed at-risk teenagers from all over the world and let them tell their own stories. We hear from two girls in war-torn Belfast, boys from a homeless shelter in Johannesburg, a Thai girl who was rescued after being sold into prostitution at eight years old, an HIV-positive young man living on the streets in San Francisco and other teens from around the world. The young people tell their stories eloquently. Most of them, while aware of the social, political and economic forces that have shaped their lives, are taking responsibility for their lives and working for a better future for themselves and others. $22.99 **Y**

Voices from the Streets: Former Gang Members Tell Their Stories

S. Beth Atkin

In this important and relevant book, Atkin probes the ways in which these young people got involved in gangs, and the crisis or inspiration that helps them to get free. The young people describe their neighborhoods, family troubles, poverty, racism and the other influences in their lives. The photographs, journal entries, poems and mainly the young people's own words will help readers understand the toll gang life takes on kids, and help adults understand what we need to change to make gang life less attractive to kids whose lives have bottomed out. $17.95 **M, Y**

Fly Away Home
Eve Bunting
Andrew and his father live in an airport. Andrew shares details of daily life, survival strategies and his hopes for a better life in this poignant look at a homeless family. $5.95 **E**

Smoky Night
Eve Bunting
This Caldecott Award winning book takes place during one night of the Los Angeles riots. Daniel and his mother watch with horror and amazement as their neighborhood shops are looted and are awakened in the night when their building catches fire. When Daniel's cat and the cat that belongs to the Korean grocer, Mrs. Kim, both get lost, they all have to wait for the cats to be rescued. When the cats show up, it turns out they've been keeping each other company the whole time. After huddling together in the night, Daniel, his mother and Mrs. Kim realize that if the cats can get together, maybe they can try to be friends also. Great illustrations and a sensitive handling of a very difficult subject.
$6.00 **P, E**

Us and Them: A History of Intolerance in America
Jim Carnes
This is an illustrated history of the United States, based around the theme of intolerance due to race, religon, ethnicity and sexual orientation. Intolerance has pervaded every era in our history, as this book clearly shows. Carnes includes photos and many documents for kids to analyze. $12.95 **M, Y**

Why Did It Happen? Helping Children Cope in a Violent World
Janice Cohn

When Daniel's friend Mr. James is held up and injured in his neighborhood market, Daniel is very upset and can't make sense of the robbery. His parents help him overcome his anger and fear, and he becomes one of the friends who come through to help this popular shopkeeper recover. Cohn also provides an introduction for adults on the ways we can help kids cope with the pervasive effects of violence in this society. $15.00   **P, E**

Checking on the Moon
Jenny Davis

Cab Jones and her grandmother must spend the summer together, even though they have never met before. The neighborhood is an old working class area of Pittsburgh, with crime on the rise. When a rape occurs, Cab participates, with neighborhood residents of all ages and ethnic backgrounds, in finding a creative and peaceful way to take back their streets. $3.99   **M, Y**

Uncle Willie and the Soup Kitchen
Dyanne DiSalvo-Ryan

The young narrator wonders why his uncle works in a soup kitchen, and he accompanies him one day. He learns that it's a friendly place and that, not only can he perform a service for others, but that the helping enriches him. $4.95   **P**

Close-Up
Szabinka Dudevszky

Fifteen teenagers living in the Netherlands, but from all around the world, tell their stories of living separated from their families. While most of the separations are due to domestic upheaval, some are political in nature. In one moving story, a girl from Iran describes how she needed to flee her country because a powerful older man wanted her as his second wife. Her family tried to protect her and faced serious and violent harassment. She finally left Iran and came alone to the Netherlands at 16. $15.95   **Y**

Lives Turned Upside Down: Homeless Children in Their Own Words and Photographs

Jim Hubbard

Jim Hubbard is founder of "Shooting Back," an organization that provides cameras and other arts media to homeless and at-risk kids, enabling them to document their world. In this book, four of those children's photos are reproduced and they talk about their lives in the streets, in a shelter and in the extreme poverty in which they live. We need to hear the voices of some of the poor children whose numbers are ever-increasing. $17.00 **P, E**

The Raging Quiet

Sherryl Jordan

In this novel set in a medieval village, 16-year-old Marnie's life is turned upside down when she is married to a much older man, who dies soon after the wedding. She befriends a young man, Raven, who is thought to be a raving lunatic by the ignorant in the village, but Marnie figures out that her new friend is deaf, and the two develop a system of sign language together. Marnie's independence, intelligence and her deepening relationship with Raven brand her a witch in the eyes of the village. Love, compassion and bravery do finally win out over ignorance and superstition. $17.00 **Y**

Fire at the Triangle Factory

Holly Littlefield

A young Jewish girl, Minnie, and her best friend, Tessa, a young Italian girl, have become fast friends over the years toiling in the horrendous working conditions at the Triangle Shirtwaist Factory. When fire breaks out in the factory, both girls need each other to escape the smoke and flames. Minnie's father's relief at finding his daughter alive and unharmed overcomes his fear of Tessa's difference when he learns of Tessa's role in saving Minnie's life. Based on the fire of March 25, 1911. $5.95 **E**

Nettie's Trip South
Ann Turner

Based on the actual childhood diary of the author's great grandmother, this is a story of a northern girl who traveled south during
the days of slavery. She records the slaves' living conditions with
horror and outrage. She eventually grew up to be an abolitionist.
$4.95 E

Homeless
Bernard Wolf

This photo essay follows an eight-year-old boy, Mikey, through
about six months of his life with his family in a transition apartment in the Henry Street Settlement Urban Family Center in
Manhattan. He is the oldest of four children, and he shares his
joys, difficulties, fears and his family's survival tactics living on
the economic edge. The book shows how the social safety net
has worked to keep this family intact through some hard times.
$16.95 E

P = preschool
E = early elementary
M = middle school
Y = young adult
AA = all ages

Strong Girls and Women:
Picture Books and Literature

Girl Goddess #9
Francesca Lia Block
Highly praised and ultra-hip writer Block has stories about many different kinds of girl goddesses, including a girl named La for her place of birth, a girl with two mothers and a fascinating assortment of other characters all making their way through a very contemporary and complex world. $4.95 **M, Y**

Dangerous Angels
Francesca Lia Block
The popular, highly acclaimed Weetzie Bat books are now collected in one volume. The saga begins when Los Angeles teenager Weetzie Bat finds a magic lamp and makes three wishes: for a duck (a boyfriend) for her best friend Dirk, "my secret agent lover man" for herself, and a house for all of them to live in. All the wishes come true, and many adventures follow. Later books involve Weetzie's daughter Cherokee Bat, her half-sister Witch Baby, Cherokee's best friend Raphael Chong Jah-Love, Witch Baby's soulmate Angel Juan and their band, the Goat Guys. Written in Francesca Lia Block's magical, unforgettable language, the Weetzie Bat books are modern-day fairy tales that celebrate the cultural and natural wonders of L.A. without overlooking problems like homophobia, AIDS, racism and poverty. $12.00 **M, Y**

Princess Smartypants
Babette Cole

Princess Smartypants has no interest in getting married. She is wild and crazy in ways that only Cole is capable of imagining. She dreams up impossible tasks for all the princes who show up to win her hand, and when a gentleman finally can complete all her wacky tasks, she still finds a way to remain blissfully independent. It is almost impossible to read this book without laughing aloud, no matter what your age. $5.99 **P, E**

Eleanor
Barbara Cooney

Eleanor Roosevelt's story is a familiar one for most adults, but this beautifully illustrated picture book introduces her to a new generation of children. The book focuses on her early life and the hardships she faced even as a child of wealth, losing both her parents before the age of ten, and having a mother who was quite cruel to her when she was alive. Her extended family and her father introduced her to the ideas of caring about those in need when she was young. Those lessons, and her painful childhood, may be what set her apart from other women of wealth and helped her to become a great champion of the rights of women and the oppressed. $5.99 **E**

Catherine Called Birdy
Karen Cushman

This is a unique look at the Middle Ages through the journal entries of a pre-feminist 14-year-old girl. Catherine's father is determined to marry her off to a noble with money, and she is equally determined to have nothing to do with the men her father has brought forth as suitors. From the opening line, this book is funny and difficult to put down. $3.95 **M**

The Midwife's Apprentice
Karen Cushman
In a second journey back to medieval England, Cushman writes about another feisty heroine in this Newbery Award winner. Brat is a girl without a home, parents or a future; she is sleeping in a farmer's dung heap when she is found by the village midwife, a difficult woman who only wants someone to do unskilled, grueling work. Alyce, as Brat eventually names herself, watches, learns, acquires a cat and becomes a midwife in her own right. $7.50 M

The Dragon in the Rocks
Marie Day
Mary Anning was a child when she began the work that would make her one of the most famous women scientists in England's history. She was fascinated with fossils on the beach and in the cliffs around her village. This picture book tells her story, including a description of the complete fossil of a huge dinosaur that Mary, still a child, laboriously chiseled out of the rock and reconstructed, and which still is exhibited in the Natural History Museum in London. $5.95 E

Juniper
Monica Furlong
This prequel to *Wise Child* tells the story of Juniper's early life; she is born a medieval princess, but not content in her pampered life, she learns the lore of healing, herbs and magic from her godmother. All too soon, she must use all her resources to prevent disaster. $4.99 M

Wise Child
Monica Furlong
In a remote Scottish village, Wise Child is taken in by healer and sorceress Juniper. Wise Child learns about herbs, reading and some magic in this unforgettable adventure. The drama of earth wisdom versus the rigidity and superstition of early Christianity is played out in this excellent novel. $4.99 M, Y

I Look Like a Girl
Sheila Hamanaka

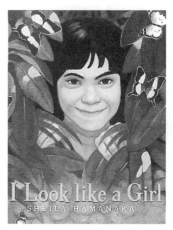

Hamanaka has written a hymn to the new generation of girls, for whom the sky is the limit! The book is one long poem reaching into the imagination of a young girl—she imagines she is really a tiger, a dolphin, a mustang and more. "Throw out those glass slippers. Send the fairies to sleep. No prince is waiting for me. For if you look twice, past the sugar and spice, the eyes of a tiger you'll see." $16.00 **P, E**

Seven Brave Women
Betsy Hearne

Why is history the study of men and wars? Why is bravery measured by actions on the battlefield? The women in this book are all brave, from the great-great-great grandmother who crossed the sea, pregnant and with two small children in a wooden boat, to the grandmother who entered a college classroom bearing the sign "no dogs, children, or women allowed," to the girl-child who sees the bravery in her foremothers and is sure she will find her own way to make history. The paintings in this book are beautiful, and the message is powerful. A great gift for a young feminist, or even an old one! $15.00 **AA**

Maria's Comet
Deborah Hopkinson

This book introduces us to Maria Mitchell, the world's first female astronomer, as a child growing up on 19th-century Nantucket. Her father has a telescope, and one night he finally lets Maria go out and sweep the sky with him. The illustrations capture the magic Maria and her father must have seen in the night sky. $16.00 **E**

The Lilith Summer
Hadley Irwin

In order to buy a bicycle, 12-year-old Ellen agrees to care for elderly Lilith for the summer. Even though it's just a job to Ellen at first, they become very close, providing Ellen and the reader with an inside view of the life of an older woman. $8.95 **M**

The Bean Trees
Barbara Kingsolver

Nineteen-year-old Taylor Greer drives as far west as her beat up VW will go, ending up in Tucson with custody of a three-year-old, and in the good company of some other memorable characters, including kindly Mattie who runs a sanctuary for Central American refugees along with her used tire shop. Taylor is a wonderful character—adults will enjoy this book too. $6.99 **Y**

Allegra Maud Goldman
Edith Konecky

In a memorable, often hilarious voice, Allegra tells of her coming of age in an affluent Jewish Brooklyn family in the 1920s. Allegra is defiant, precocious, lively and highly intelligent; she tells of her family and of her complicated love for them. Three generations in our family fell in love with this book. $12.95 **M, Y**

Girls to the Rescue Series
Edited by Bruce Lansky

Writer, performer and storyteller Lansky worked with 75 girls ages eight to 13 to select ten stories for each book, both original and adapted from folktales, featuring "clever, courageous girls from around the world." These popular books are easy to read and lots of fun; it's great to see these collections at a low price for distribution to lots of kids! There are six books in the series so far.
$3.95 EACH **E, M**

She's Wearing a Dead Bird on Her Head
Kathryn Lasky

Minna Hall and Harriet Hemenway were two upper-class Bostonian women around the turn of the century. They were disgusted with the increasing reliance in women's fashion on feathers of exotic birds and even whole birds on the hats that were worn every day. These women mobilized women and men of Boston society, and even educated schoolchildren, to assist in stopping the slaughter of birds. Their success in founding the Audubon society is in evidence to this day—the organization is still working to protect birds. $5.95 **P, E**

Nobody Owns the Sky: The Story of
Brave Bessie Coleman
Reeve Lindbergh

In a colorful picture book, Lindbergh tells the story of this pioneer who was determined to overcome both the gender barrier and the race barrier and become an airplane pilot. This was an amazing feat in the early part of the century, especially considering that an overwhelming majority of airplane pilots are still white men today. The book is in rhyming verse, with colorful paintings by Pamela Paparone. $5.99 **P, E**

Ballot Box Battle
Emily Arnold McCully

Most girls growing up in the new millennium will find it difficult to believe that women were not allowed to vote so recently in history. This picture book tells the story of a girl whose neighbor and friend is the suffragette Elizabeth Cady Stanton, and the act of bravery this friendship inspires. $6.99 **E**

The Bobbin Girl
Emily Arnold McCully

Ten-year-old Rebecca is working in a cotton mill to help her family. Based on the memoirs of a real mill girl from Lowell, Massachusetts, this book recreates early factory conditions for children, showing how the owners exploited the powerless positions of the all female workforce, most of whom were laboring to escape extreme poverty or support elderly or sick relatives. When a woman Rebecca admires tries to organize a work stoppage in the face of a pay cut, many of the women feel incapable of joining in because their lives are precarious at best, but the attempt opens a whole new world of possibility for Rebecca. $5.99 **M**

Mirette on the High Wire

Emily Arnold McCully

Mirette is the daughter of a boarding-house owner whose patrons are largely perfomers. When mysterious Bellini appears at the boarding house, and strings a high wire behind the boarding house, Mirette is hooked. She wants to do nothing more than learn to perform on the wire. Bellini hesitates at first, but he is impressed by Mirette's skills and determination. Finally, it is Mirette who helps Bellini overcome his fear of the wire. McCully won a Caldecott medal for the watercolor illustrations of Paris. $5.99 **P, E**

Molly Bannaky

Alice McGill

At the age of 17, Molly Walsh narrowly escaped death for "stealing" when the lord of the English manorhouse where she worked as a dairy maid prosecuted her because the cow kicked over a bucket of milk! Instead, she was shipped over to Maryland as a seven-year indentured servant. After her work ended, she became a farmer in her own right. For assistance, she purchased a slave, Bannaky, and promised to set him free as soon as her land was

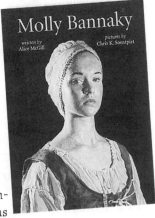

cleared. The two fell in love, wed and raised four daughters. The son of the eldest, Benjamin Bannaker, became a brilliant and reknowned astronomer, famous to this day. The paintings by Chris K. Soentpiet are powerful and detailed, with every page illustrating the pride and strength of Molly and Bannaky. $16.00 **E**

The Wise Woman and Her Secret
Eve Merriam

In a modern fable, a wise elderly woman lives alone, but many people come to seek the secret of her wisdom and make it their own. As people hunt for an easily acquired secret that will make them wise, one girl spends time observing her natural environment, and when she approaches the wise woman, it is apparent that she has begun the journey to true wisdom. $5.99 **P, E**

The Paper Bag Princess
Robert Munsch

The classic anti-fairy tale, and a popular kids' book. Elizabeth, dressed in only a paper bag, outsmarts a marauding dragon to rescue her fiance the Prince, with a surprising twist at the end. $5.95 **P, E**

The King's Equal
Katherine Paterson

In an original tale, the selfish and cruel Prince Raphael learns a hard-won lesson, thanks to the wise Rosamund and a magical wolf. The story is another wonderful addition to the modern genre of anti-sexist fairy tales. Beautiful illustrations by the Russian artist Vladmir Vagin. $6.95 **P, E**

Lyddie
Katherine Paterson

Lyddie works hard all day long on the farm, but when her family gives up their land to pay a debt, she sets off for the mills of Lowell, Massachusetts, to help them get back on their feet. She meets strong-willed young women, some of whom are organizing to improve the near slavery conditions in the mills. A fascinating look at New England in the 1840s. $4.99 **M, Y**

Jojo's Flying Side Kick
Brian Pinkney
This book is fun and unique, about a young girl working to earn her yellow belt. Jojo needs to break a board with her kick; she is afraid not only of her test but also of the tree outside her window. Her hard work, creativity and support from her parents and grandfather help her succeed. Acclaimed illustrator Pinkney creates an adorable Jojo and a convincingly scary tree spirit. $5.99 **P, E**

The Princess and the Admiral
Charlotte Pomerantz
In a story derived from a Vietnamese legend, a wise princess nonviolently outsmarts the attackers who threaten her kingdom with a huge fleet of fighting ships. $8.95 **E**

Fearless Girls, Wise Women and Beloved Sisters: Heroines in Folktales from Around the World
Kathleen Ragan
There are many other collections of folktales for strong girls and women, but Kathleen Ragan has collected more than 100 tales in this volume, and the range of cultures is phenomenal. Stories hale from Turkey, Iraq, Lesotho, Micronesia, Korea and Romania, to name only a few of the origins. The bravery, intelligence and survival skills shown by the main characters in these tales is astounding and varies greatly with the culture, making these stories all the more interesting. $15.95 **E, M, Y**

Cut From the Same Cloth: American Women of Myth, Legend and Tall Tale
Robert San Souci
The author brings together 15 tales from all regions and many of the cultures of this country. Most of these tales will be brand new to the reader, as heroines are still not the norm in folktales. Heroines include Annie Christmas, a New Orleans dock worker, who

was, it was said "six feet eight inches tall, black as coal, weighed over 250 pounds and was fearless," and the goddess Hiiaka from Hawaiian legend. Expressive woodcuts by Brian Pinkney illustrate each story. $8.99 **E, M**

Stay True: Short Stories for Strong Girls

Edited by Marilyn Singer

Eleven top authors write stories for young adolescents, all with characters who are grappling with the issues of growing up and staying true to yourself. They explore issues of independence, family ties, sexual abuse and relationships, to name a few. $4.99 **Y**

Shabanu, Daughter of the Wind

Suzanne Fisher Staples

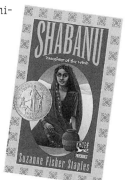

Shabanu lives with her traditional Muslim family in the Cholistan desert in contemporary Pakistan. Because she is the free-spirited youngest daughter, her parents have let her be a little freer than most girls are allowed to be, but all that may change when, to ensure her family's survival, she may have to marry a man old enough to be her grandfather. Suzanne Fisher Staples is a wonderful writer; Shabanu's suspenseful, moving story shows us a culture that is different from anything most Americans have ever experienced. $4.99 **M**

Haveli

Suzanne Fisher Staples

In this sequel to *Shabanu, Daughter of the Wind*, Shabanu continues to be a woman of honor and integrity living in an impossible situation in modern Pakistani society. She is also a young mother to a baby daughter. They are in grave danger; the older wives of Shabanu's husband are constantly threatening both Shabanu and the baby.

Shabanu wants nothing more or less than to raise her child in the Cholistan desert, where she was raised, but there are many obstacles in her way. As a woman in a traditional Muslim country, Shabanu is nearly powerless. To read *Haveli* is to journey thousands of miles to another place and to what seems like another time, but is not. $4.99 **Y**

The Gardener
Sarah Stewart

There is nothing outrageous or flamboyant about Lydia Grace, an intelligent, creative, determined young girl sent from her rural home to live and work with her unsmiling uncle at his bakery in a stark city during the Depression. Lydia Grace carries with her a love of gardening and her seed packages. When she sees empty window boxes and an unused flat roof, she knows just what to do! She creates a garden spot, sharing knowledge of gardening and learning about baking. The Caldecott Honor illustrations by David Small are deceptively simple, revealing details anew at every reading. $5.95 **P, E**

The Forest Wife
Theresa Tomlinson

Mary has grown up in a castle and is desperate to escape a terrible arranged marriage. Her nursemaid, Agnes, helps her escape into the forest, where Agnes's true skills are revealed. She is a healer and wise woman, helping many escape the greed and unfair punishments of landholders. Mary observes and matures, and is involved in exciting adventures, eventually becoming the Maid Marian of the Robin Hood legend. $4.99 **M**

Kate Shelley and the Midnight Express
Margaret Wetterer

Based on an historic incident in 1881, Kate's bravery saved hundreds of people from drowning when she undertook a perilous journey to warn the train operators that a bridge was out from a terrible storm. $5.95 **E**

Not One Damsel in Distress: World Folktales for Strong Girls

Jane Yolen

This book highlights Jane Yolen's extraordinary story-telling skills. Thirteen tales from cultures around the globe tell of girls and women who are crafty, brave, inspired, compassionate and strong—anything but sleeping beauties. Yolen's book is dedicated to her daughter and granddaughters, but the dedication could be written by many of us, ending in the words "I never knew their stories when I was your age. Not in real life. Not in folklore. But I do now." $17.00   **E, M**

Dragon Soup

Arlene Williams

In an original fable, Tonlu tries to steal one pearl from the dragons who live in the nearby mountains. If she is successful, her family will avoid the terrible choice of losing their farm or losing Tonlu in marriage to a wealthy merchant. The dragons awaken as she is taking one pearl; she is terrified by their talk of dragon soup, until she realizes that they want her to judge which dragon makes the better soup! She wisely figures a way for everyone to win, and enriches her life in the process. $15.95   **M**

Fairy Tale Collections Featuring Strong Women and Girls

These collections are all popular gift books. They are great for reading aloud to elementary age children, for older kids to read to themselves and for adults who want a good read. Some of the tales will be familiar, but in most the reader will discover completely unknown additions to the tradition of fairy tales, a tradition too long dominated by Disney's distorted interpretations.

Maid of the North

Ethel Phelps $8.95   **E, M**

Tatterhood and Other Tales

Ethel Phelps $9.95 **E, M**

Womenfolk and Fairy Tales

Rosemary Minard $18.00 **E, M**

Don't Bet on the Prince

Jack Zipes
Included here are both the tales themselves and
commentaries from feminist writers. $18.99 **M, Y**

P = preschool
E = early elementary
M = middle school
Y = young adult
AA = all ages

Strong Girls and Women: History and Current Issues

Finding Our Way: The Teen Girls' Survival Guide
Allison Abner and Linda Villarosa

This book is directed at girls in their early to middle teens, and it received rave reviews from Mary Pipher as well as the teenagers we know who have read it. In addition to the information it provides about healthy insides, good bodies and sex, the book talks about issues like sexism, racism and abusive relationships. This is all presented in an interesting, approachable style. $13.50 **Y**

America's Champion Swimmer: Gertrude Ederle
David A. Adler

From the time Ederle was a young child, she was an exceptional swimmer and loved the water. At 16, in the early 1920s, she swam 17 miles off Manhattan, beating the men's record. After winning three gold metals at the 1924 Olympics, she set her sights on the English Channel. The length and roughness of the water made this goal nearly impossible. Ederle attempted one crossing, but was halted by her coach, against her will, before reaching her goal. Her second attempt was successful, swimming through a brutal storm in the Channel, and arriving a hero to women around the world. This picture book is sure to appeal to all kids, as the story is exciting and well told and the illustrations are clear and expressive. $16.00 **P, E**

Extraordinary Girls
Maya Ajmera, Olateju Omoludun and Sarah Strunk

This beautiful book profiles exceptional girls from all over the world. Their successes in a variety of fields are interesting and inspiring, and the photographs are gorgeous. $16.95 **E**

Girls: A History of Growing Up Female in America
Penny Colman

Many books tell us about what women have done, but this book only looks at the lives of girls of the many cultures that comprise this country, from the earliest known history to the present. There are many historic photographs and drawings of girls at play and work, including a photo of newly freed slave girls, and a heart-breaking picture of Native American students at an Indian school being trained to work for white families. The author heavily quotes from letters and journals of girls regarding the Underground Railroad, the journey west, immigration and much more. Any page of this book contains fascinating information. $18.95 **E, M**

A Heart in Politics: Jeanette Rankin and Patsy Mink
Sue Davidson

This biography tells the story of two pioneers in United States politics. Rankin was the first woman to run for Congress and devoted her career to working for peace, suffrage and social change. Mink, a Japanese woman from Hawaii, was the first nonwhite woman in the Senate and a vocal advocate for legislation benefiting women. $9.95 **M**

Getting the Real Story: Nellie Bly and Ida B. Wells
Sue Davidson

Two biographies in one, of two independent news reporters around the turn of the century. Nellie Bly went into prisons, mental institutions and very poor neighborhoods in disguise and wrote about what she saw, astounding the nation and forcing big changes to be made in the places whose seamy sides she exposed. Ida B. Wells opened people's eyes to the horrors of lynching even after her press was destroyed by the Ku Klux Klan, and despite death threats. $8.95 **M**

Deal With It! A Whole New Approach to Your Body, Brain and Life as a Gurl

Esther Drill

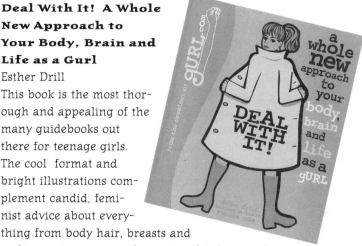

This book is the most thorough and appealing of the many guidebooks out there for teenage girls. The cool format and bright illustrations complement candid, feminist advice about everything from body hair, breasts and making out, to money, depression, birth control, schoolwork and much, much more. This is a fun book that young teenagers will enjoy and many adults will wish had been written years ago. $15.00 **Late M, Y**

Eleanor Roosevelt: A Life of Discovery

Russell Friedman

This book is perfect for middle-school-aged kids, with a fascinating description of Roosevelt's entire life—from her difficult childhood to her awakening to herself as a public figure, through her activist life after Franklin's death. $10.95 **M**

Brave New Girls: Creative Ideas to Help Girls Be Confident, Healthy and Happy

Jeanette Gadeberg

We have sold many copies of this book to folks working with girls, and to parents. Topics this book covers include friends, body image, family, money, getting things done and other areas girls can explore through writing, thinking and exercises. $12.95 **M**

Period
JoAnn Gardner-Loulan
A great book on menstruation, full of humorous pictures and friendly, supportive advice and information. $9.95 **M**

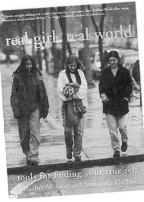

Real Girl, Real World: Tools for Finding Your True Self
Heather M. Gray and Samantha Phillips
Seal Press, a women-run and owned press, published this excellent, feminist look at the issues of adolescence. This is a highly readable book, with great information and wonderful additional resources throughout the book, instead of confining them to a list at the end of the book that only the most committed reader will encounter. They describe the commercial origins of shaving body hair and the cult of thinness, essentials about sex, gender roles and much, much more. $14.95 **M, Y**

Women of Hope: African Americans Who Made a Difference
Joyce Hansen
This beautiful book contains photo-essays on the many African-American women who have inspired us all through their bravery, lives in the arts, education and other areas. The black and white portraits and the writing are superb. $16.95 **M**

Up in the Air: The Story of Bessie Coleman
Philip Hart
Bessie Coleman grew up in the early 1900s in Texas; she was responsible for watching her younger sisters while her mother worked as a domestic. Even when she had to pick cotton in sum-mer, she had her mind set on more education and a better life. Early in her adulthood, she discovered her dream and followed her ambition with all her abilities—she wanted to be the first African-American woman to fly an airplane. The photographs and

text in this book tell the story of the dawn of the airplane and also show us how black women lived in that time of great change, the early 1900s. $6.95 **E, M**

Amazing Women in American History: A Book of Answers for Kids
Sue Heinemann

This New York Public Library reference book answers questions including "When did women start going to college?" "Did any southern women speak out against slavery?" and hundreds of others. In addition, there are boxes of text about such events as the Triangle Shirtwaist Fire, and Isadora Duncan's dancing. $12.95 **E, M**

Everygirl's Guide to Feminism
Kate Hughes

The history and philosophies of feminism are explained in this attractive, easy-to-understand guide. Included are chapters on common myths, bodies, relationships and the workplace. At the end of the book is a glossary explaining a wide range of names and terms, everything from Ecofeminism to Sigmund Freud to liposuction to the Spice Girls. $9.95 **M, Y**

It's a Girl Thing: How to Stay Healthy, Safe and in Charge
Mavis Jukes

This book is written with preteens and early teens in mind, covering such areas as bras, boys, periods and more from a sensible, feminist perspective. This book is fun and attractive; most girls will probably want to pick it up and peruse. $5.99 **M, Y**

Growing Up: It's a Girl Thing
Mavis Jukes

This is an edition of the excellent *It's a Girl Thing* written for younger girls, from eight to 11, with frank and simple information about body changes, periods, acceptable touching and all that goes along with the above. $10.00 **M**

Scholastic Encyclopedia of Women in the United States
Sheila Keenan

This book mainly contains annotated biographies, along with photographs and drawings, about hundreds of notable women in American history. The arrangement is chronological, with an overview of women's lives, rights and political movements in different historical periods. The women selected are an eclectic lot, not all of whom supported women's rights, but all have been instrumental in politics, the arts, education or some other important field. $17.95 **M, Y**

Mother Jones: One Woman's Fight for Labor
Betsy Harvey Kraft

Generously illustrated with period photographs and newspaper drawings, this biography is full of information and anecdotes rarely available to young people. Mother Jones brought attention to child laborers, miners and other workers; she led an active, political life well into her nineties. $16.95 **E, M**

A Whole New Ball Game: The Story of the All-American Girls Professional Baseball League
Sue Macy

Anyone who is interested in the history of women's sports, who loved *A League of Their Own*, or who is a baseball fan will want to read this book and look through the photos and paraphernalia from the league and its 12 seasons. $4.99 **M**

Sisters in Strength: American Women Who Made a Difference
Yona Zeldis McDonough

A striking red cover with bright, folk-art-style portraits of the 11 women profiled in this book makes the reader want to dive in and discover who these women were. The author writes a three-page biography of each of the women, and Malcah Zeldis, the talented illustrator, lavishly adds to each woman's tale with multiple painted scenes from each life. The selection of women is limited to the truly famous, and mostly white, but the writing and artwork will inspire some kids to learn more about the accomplishments of these and other women in history. $16.00 **E**

Cool Women: The Thinking Girl's Guide to the Hippest Women in History
Pam Nelson

Widely diverse women from a huge variety of places and times are profiled here, from the Amazons to Josephine Baker to Wu Zhao to Margaret Sanger and many, many more. The format is colorful and fun, and many girls will be alternately inspired and shocked by these famous and notorious women. $19.95 **E, M**

Ophelia Speaks
Sarah Shandler

The author, now in college, was inspired as a teenager by Mary Pipher's *Reviving Ophelia* to collect stories from all over the country about life as a teenage girl. With chapters on family relationships, drugs, eating, sexuality, school, religion and feminism, this book will help teenage girls see that they are not alone in dealing with the many problems of adolescence. This is also a good book for parents who want to better understand the problems their daughters face. $14.00 **M, Y**

Inspirations: Stories of Women Artists
Leslie Sills

Georgia O'Keefe, Frida Kahlo, Alice Neel and Faith Ringgold, four very different but all incredibly talented women artists, are profiled here. Each section includes a generous sampling of color reproductions of the artist's work. Each of these women is truly an inspiration. $17.95 **E, M**

Visions: Stories of Women Artists
Leslie Sills

In a companion volume to *Inspirations*, Sills has profiled four more talented and visionary women artists: Mary Cassatt, Betye Saar, Leonora Carrington and Mary Frank. Each woman has a very different style, uses different media and conveys different messages and emotions through her work. These volumes are as essential today as they were 20 years ago—there is still very little published about women in the arts for young readers. This book is illustrated with high-quality color plates, and the text is fascinating. We hope Sills will continue discovering wonderful women artists for years to come. $18.95 **E, M**

Girls Think of Everything:
Stories of Inventions by Women
Catherine Thimmesh
Inside the front and back covers of this book is an informative and surprising timeline of inventions by women, from the invention in 3000 B.C. by His-ling-shi of a method of gathering and weaving silk, through the 1892 invention of the street-cleaning cart, to Georgena Terry's 1992 bicycle seat for women. Inside, the book is full of stories of women's and girls' creativity, inventing many of the items we take for granted. Any girl with a desire to be an inventor will love this book. $16.00 **E, M**

Georgia O'Keefe
Robyn Montana Turner
This book follows O'Keefe from Sun Prairie, Wisconsin, to her life in New York, to her arrival in New Mexico, where she finally felt at home. Her work, professional successes and styles are all profiled in this interesting book. $8.95 **M**

Young Oxford History of Women in the United States
For an amazing look at the history of American women, check out this new eleven-volume set. The books are full of graphic illustrations, all written by experts in that historic era. $9.95 EACH **M**

1 The Tried and the True: Native-American Women Confronting Colonization
John Demos

2 The Colonial Mosaic: 1600–1760
Jane Kamensky

3 Limits of Independence: 1760–1800
Marilyn Salmon

4 Breaking New Ground: 1800–1848
Michael Goldberg

5 Unfinished Battle: 1848–1865
Harriet Sigerman

6 Laborers for Liberty: 1865– 1890
Harriet Sigerman

7 New Paths to Power: 1890–1920
Karen Manners Smith

8 From Ballots to Breadlines: 1920–1940
Sarah Jane Deutsch

9 Pushing the Limits: 1940–1961
Elaine Taylor May

10 The Road to Equality: 1962–present
William H. Chafe

11 Biographical Supplement
Harriet Sigerman   ($11.95)

P = preschool
E = early elementary
M = middle school
Y = young adult
AA = all ages

Changing Boys:
Challenging Stereotypes

Note: This section contains only a few books, because few books are published for and about boys who are different, who may have what are considered "sissy" characteristics. Many excellent books in other sections feature brave, strong, principled, outspoken, creative, brilliant, sensitive and kind boys and men. These books listed in this section explore gender roles as they relate to boys, some with humor and some seriously.

Prince Cinders
Babette Cole
Babette Cole has written some of the funniest role-reversal books ever, in which she pokes fun at traditional fairy tales. In this one, Prince Cinders lives with "three big hairy brothers who were always teasing him about his looks." When he encounters a princess at the bus stop, he manages to leave his trousers behind instead of a glass slipper. Cole's illustrations are as humorous and outlandish as her writing and concepts. Sure to be a hit.
$5.99 **P, E**

Toestomper and the Caterpillars
Sharleen Collicott
Toestomper is a classic bully. He hangs out with his friends, the Rowdy Ruffians, cheats at cards and is generally "mean, rude and disgusting." When Toestomper finds a group of helpless, blue, fuzzy caterpillars who need him, he gradually begins to change. As he begins helping his blue friends, at first with reluctance, but gradually with enthusiasm, his old friends are appalled. At one point, the Rowdy Ruffians call Toestomper a sissy for hanging

out with "little blue bugs." The book ends with Toestomper and his caterpillars winning at cards against the Rowdy Ruffians! The author has also wonderfully illustrated this colorful, funny story about a bully changing his ways. $15.00 **P, E**

The Teenage Guy's Survival Guide: The Real Deal on Girls, Growing Up and Other Guy Stuff
Jeremy Daldry

This appealing, reassuring book brings lots of information to boys in a friendly, readable format. A large section on relationships focuses on relationships with girls, but also includes a smaller but accepting and helpful section for boys who feel they may be, or are, gay. There is basic information about asking a girl out, how and when to kiss, what rejection feels like and more. Other sections provide insight into body changes, the emotional roller coaster and social life. This author recommends a good cry when necessary, and he counsels boys to be respectful and honest with girls. The book uses humor effectively to lighten up some of the potentially heavy subject matter. Highly recommended. $8.95 **M, Y**

Oliver Button Is a Sissy
Tomie DePaola

This is an older book, but it remains one of the few books that brings out the issue of boys who don't fit the macho-boy stereotype. Oliver Button's favorite activity is dancing. He loves dance school, practicing and performing, and hates playing anything with a ball. He maintains his integrity in the face of teasing in school, and when he dances his best in a talent show, the school grafitti is altered from "Oliver Button is a Sissy" to "Oliver Button is a Star." $5.95 **P, E**

Ira Sleeps Over
Bernard Waber

Ira has a problem. He is about to sleep at his best friend's house for the first time, and he wants to bring his nightly sleeping companion, his teddy bear. His parents encourage him, but his older sister assures him that Reggie will tease him mercilessly. He worries all day that Reggie will think he is a baby if he brings his bear along. In the end, of course, Ira is not the only boy who sleeps with a teddy bear. This book has been around for many years, but it is still fresh and fun to read. $6.95 **P, E**

Justin and the Best Biscuits in the World
Mildred Pitts Walter

When Justin visits his grandfather's ranch he learns about mending fences, black cowboys and handling horses, but he also learns some useful skills to bring home, like making biscuits and organizing his room. A good portrait of a boy's feelings about being the only male in the family. $4.99 **E**

Science and Nature

P = preschool
E = early elementary
M = middle school
Y = young adult
AA = all ages

Alejandro's Gift

Richard E. Albert

Alejandro lives in a desert in the Southwest, with only his burro for companionship. When he plants a garden, he observes the small creatures of the desert emerge, taking advantage of the water and shade he has provided. He then undertakes a major project, building a waterhole, for the larger animals of the desert. When his project is completed, he finds that he has enriched his life as much as his project has aided the wildlife around him. An illustrated description of the animals of the desert is provided at the end of the book. $6.95 **P, E**

Books by

Barbara Bash Bash is a terrific nature artist, and all her books are full of information, presented in an interesting and fun manner.

In the Heart of the Village:
The World of the Indian Banyan Tree

The great banyan tree in the center of a small Indian village is a place for laughing and bartering, conversing and resting, romping and chasing. Bash paints a vivid picture of its importance to the people and other animals that flourish beneath and within its welcoming branches, showing the interconnectedness of life in a rural culture. $16.95 **P**

Shadows of the Night: The Hidden World of the Little Brown Bat

A wonderful book, guaranteed to improve the image of the bat with anyone willing to give these important and intelligent creatures a chance! Includes pictures and information about baby bats.
$16.95 **P, E**

Ancient Ones: The World of the Old-Growth Douglas Fir

As with all the books in Bash's "tree tales" series, this one does a great job of showing how these massive trees are crucial for a large number of living things. This series is a terrific introduction to the concept of interdependency. $16.95 **E**

Tree of Life: The World of the African Baobab

A great introduction to the ecosystem of the African plains.
$5.95 **E**

Desert Giant: The World of the Saguaro Cactus

This cactus shelters, feeds, and supports a remarkable number of animals and plants, not least of all the local human population.
$5.95 **E**

xxxx

Stellaluna

Janell Cannon

An absolutely wonderful story features a young bat who is separated from her mother. She comes to rest in a nest of young birds, and while they can become fast friends, they see that bat food, sleep times and other habits aren't quite compatible with permanent life together. The illustrations are great, and the birds' and bats' differences are highlighted in a way that kids won't even know they are learning! $14.95 **P, E**

A River Ran Wild
Lynne Cherry

What a book! The natural history of the Nashua River, which runs through northern Massachusetts and southern New Hampshire, is told through breathtaking paintings and fascinating text. The river's evolution from pristine home to native people, flora and fauna to industrial sewer, and now to a recovering river, is a great lesson in history and ecology, as well as a book kids will cherish for the wonderful illustrations and hopeful end. $16.00 **E**

The Great Kapok Tree
Lynne Cherry

In the Amazon rainforest, a man is chopping down a Kapok tree. In a simple story with lavish illustrations, the animals and a Yanomamo boy enlighten the man about value of the rainforest. This book is truly magnificent! $6.00 **P, E**

Come Back, Salmon
Molly Cone

This excellent book follows an elementary school determined to clean up a brook that many people think is past saving. The kids work hard and are remarkably successful. $7.95 **E**

And Then There Was One:
The Mysteries of Extinction
Margery Facklam

The author discusses both naturally occurring and human caused extinctions and describes ways people have rescued species on the brink of extinction. $5.95 **E, M**

On the Day You were Born
Debra Frasier

"On the day you were born the earth turned toward your morning sky whirling past darkness, spinning the night into light." A great introduction for very small children to the sun, moon, tides, wind

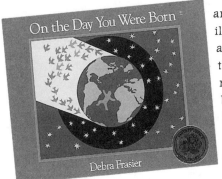

and our place among them. The illustrations are stylized, bright and attractive, and there are further explanations for the older or more curious at the end of the book. This book is a perfect new baby gift. $15.00 **P**

Jaguarundi
Virginia Hamilton

Rundi Jaguarundi is content in the wild rainforest, but as strangers come and begin cutting the forest, Rundi and the other rainforest animals need to come to a decision about whether to stay or to leave and try to find a more unbroken stretch of forest. Many rainforest animals get into the discussion, giving readers a look at the struggles currently going on. $4.99 **E**

Phoenix Rising
Karen Hesse

A thought-provoking novel looks at how a nuclear meltdown from a plant in Vermont would affect New England. Most of the story takes place on a quiet sheep farm just outside the contamination zone, but even there the effects are profound. Thirteen-year-old Nyle is not happy when she discovers that her grandmother has taken the unpopular step of housing two of the sick, who were contaminated by the fallout. Her complex relationship with 15-year-old Ezra and his mother, which wakens many of her feelings about the other losses in her life, and the backdrop of government inaction even in the face of the loss of Southern New England, make for powerful reading. $4.99 **M, Y**

How the Forest Grew
William Jaspersohn

How did a hardwood forest come about? This book takes a look at a typical New England forest—from the time it was cleared 200 years ago and abandoned when the farm family moved on, until the current stage when it is a mature forest. The illustrations clearly show the trees, wildlife and smaller plants comprising the different forest stages. This book is fascinating and informative, riveting and yet short and simple. $4.95 **P, E**

Fernando's Gift/El Regalo de Fernando
Douglas Keister
Fernando lives in the heart of the Costa Rican rainforest, in a magnificent spot. His father and grandfather know all about the plants and animals of the rainforest and are working to protect the forest. When Fernando's friend brings him to her favorite climbing tree, they discover that someone has cut the tree down. His father provides them with a young tree to plant to replace the tree that was lost. Beautiful photographs illustrate the book, giving the reader a real sense of life in the rainforest. Bilingual in Spanish and English. $6.95 **E**

Song for the Ancient Forest
Nancy Luenn
In an original tale, Raven sings and the world lives harmoniously, until the time when Europeans come and begin clear-cutting and selling trees. Raven tries to warn people of the outcome, but none can hear him. When a young girl is able to hear him, he tells her of his concerns for the world. She understands, and we hope the process of destruction has been stalled or reversed. $14.95 **E**

Story of a Dolphin
Katherine Orr
Based an a true story from the Caribbean island of Providenciales, this tale is about a dolphin who, for some unknown reason, decides to live in a harbor frequented by people. The child-narrator's father and the dolphin become close companions and are able to educate the local people in the many ways to interact with the dolphin in ways that protect both themselves and the marine mammal. $6.95 **P, E**

My Grandpa and the Sea

Katherine Orr

Grandpa is a traditional fisherman on the island of St. Lucia. As the large boats overfish the waters around the island, Grandpa is forced out of business. After much thought, he finds an ecologically sound solution to the dilemma of wanting to work on the sea but not wanting to be part of the fishing industry's destructive techniques. $5.95 **P, E**

Books by

Joanne Ryder *Illustrated by Lynne Cherry.* This outstanding series allows children to understand the life of creatures from their perspective—each of the books helps kids imagine shrinking to the size of the animal featured.

Where the Butterflies Grow

Imagine being a caterpillar, then making a cocoon and then flying high in the air and landing on flowers to find food. $15.99 **P, E**

Chipmunk Song

"Imagine you are someone small sleeping on a bed of leaves." Lynne Cherry's magnificent illustrations show a small child following a chipmunk on her daily late-summer routine. $5.99 **P**

Snail's Spell

"Imagine you are small and have no bones. Imagine you are gray, the color of smoke." In this book, kids are sent on an imaginary journey with a small boy who spends his day the size of a snail. What a delightful way to learn! $5.99 **P**

xxxx

The Lorax
Dr. Seuss
Classic environmental tale about the destruction of an ecosystem by unthinking consuming, told in Seuss's unmatched style. This book has generated controversy in its use in some schools, as the story clearly challenges children to become the stewards of the environment. $14.00 **AA**

Eco-Women: Protectors of the Earth
Willow Ann Sirch
What a great idea! The author profiles some of the women who have devoted their lives to saving our natural resources, including Marjory Stoneman Douglas, who at 106 years old was still speaking out for the preservation of the Everglades, Rachel Carson, Wangari Maathai from Kenya, a pioneer of the Green Belt Movement, and five other women of courage. This is an inspiring and essential book for anyone who wonders what they can do to work for the environment. $15.95 **E, M**

Welcome to the Green House
Jane Yolen
Yolen's poetic prose and Laura Regan's lush illustrations introduce life in the rainforest's unique ecosystem to young children. The ocelot, lizards, golden toads and kinkajous all make their appearance in a book that should help children understand why we must protect this valuable resource. $5.99 **P, E**

Save My Rainforest
Monica Zak
Omar Castillo wrote to the Mexican President about saving the rainforest, but he didn't listen. So Omar walked 870 miles with a banner and a pack of clothes to save the rainforest himself. Based on a true story and set in the present day. Beautiful illustrations.
$14.95 **P, E**

Books for Parents and Teachers

Teaching for Diversity and Social Justice:
A Sourcebook
Maurianne Adams, Lee Anne Bell, Pat Griffin
This book is the synthesis of years of work on ways of bringing
social justice into the classroom. Students and teachers examine
the many issues of oppression in our society and are led through
creative and exciting exercises examining racism, anti-Semitism,
ableism, classism and heterosexism. The authors also write about
the theory behind their ideas and include a long, thorough resource
list. This book is meant for upper-level high-school classes and
college classes. $19.95

How Schools Shortchange Girls: The AAUW Report:
A Study of Major Findings on Girls and Education
American Association of University Women
This report has spawned writing, thinking, discussion and action
all over the country; it documents the pervasiveness of gender bias
in schools and could be the first step toward ending this monumen-
tal problem. $14.95

Teaching for Social Justice:
A Democracy and Education Reader
William Ayers, Jean Ann Hunt, Therese Quinn
Combining personal stories and hands-on ideas for teaching and
writings about education by different progressive activists, this
book is a fascinating blend. It covers topics ranging from people's
recollections of life-changing experiences when they went to school
to an article on "The Global Sweatshop." $18.95

Rise Up Singing
Peter Blood
Here is an exciting collection of over 1,200 songs about feminism, labor, social change, childhood, nature and many other fun and interesting topics. Includes lyrics and guitar chords (not sheet music). $17.95

Books by
Joseph Bruchac and Michael J. Caduto All of these wonderful books are written in the same format: they contain traditional Native-American stories supplemented with creative activities for use in elementary school classrooms.

Keepers of the Animals: Native-American Stories and Wildlife Activities for Children
$19.95

Keepers of the Earth: Native-American Stories with Environmental Activities for Children
With John Kahionhes $19.95

Keepers of Life: Discovering Plants Through Native-American Stories and Earth Activities for Children $9.95

Keepers of the Night: Native-American Stories and Nocturnal Activities for Children
With David Kanietakeron Fadden $15.95

xxxx

Who's Calling the Shots?
How to Respond Effectively to Kids' Fascination
with War Play and War Toys

Nancy Carlsson-Paige and Diane Levin

This is an extensive and well-researched examination of the different ways children's play and other behavior is affected by violence
in the media. The authors see a wide gap between creative play,
which is a healthy outlet for aggression, and play scripted by T.V.,
in which kids use high-tech marketing paraphernalia as toys.
They offer ideas for helping parents encourage their kids to reclaim
play, counter stereotypes and move away from the commercial
world of T.V. toys. This book is older and does not cover the new
generation of multi-media toys, but the ideas are even more
important now. $14.95

Thirty-Three Multicultural Tales to Tell

Pleasant DeSpain

This excellent collection of stories from around the world is geared
toward anyone who wants to learn how to become a better storyteller. The stories are nonsexist and chosen for their universal
appeal. Our only complaint is that the author identifies the countries of origin of all the stories except those taken from Africa.
$15.00

Of Many Colors: Portraits of Multiracial Families

Peggy Gillespie, photos by Gigi Kaeser

This book is a compilation of a traveling photo exhibit. There is
wide range of racial diversity both within and among the families
included. Each family is photographed and then interviewed by the
author. A great book for adults and to share with children. $19.95

Voices of a Generation: Teenage Girls Report About Their Lives Today
Pamela Haag

In 1997 and 1998, the American Association of University women held summits across the country for girls ages 11 to 17. This book is a compilation of their thoughts on the most important challenges facing teenage girls; included are both survey results, broken down by race and age, and quotations from anonymous girls, identified by age, race and home city. The results show the new ways girls today are thinking about issues like identity, peer pressure, sex and academic achievement. Some of the comments will be surprising to adults, and many provide insight about the roles adults can play in helping girls through adolescence. $13.95

Boys Will Be Men: Raising our Sons for Courage, Caring and Commitment
Paul Kivel

Kivel recognizes the need for a new kind of man in our society; his insights will help parents and educators understand their own ideas about masculinity and begin learning how to raise thoughtful, caring, nonviolent boys. This book forces us all to examine the many assumptions we bring to our interactions with boys and where these assumptions come from. A great resource for boys, men and anyone who works or lives with them. $16.95

The Schools Our Children Deserve: Moving Beyond Traditional Classrooms and "Tougher Standards"
Alfie Kohn

In this book, acclaimed writer Alfie Kohn addresses many of the current controversies facing educators today. He explains the problems with calls for "back to basics" and "tougher standards" and argues that schools need to focus on content and process instead of achievement, active instead of passive learning and creativity instead of conformity to standards. A wide variety of child development research and educational theory is included to support Kohn's arguments and to show that our school systems are in need of serious changes, and Kohn provides suggestions for parents and teachers who want to begin implementing these changes in their schools. $24.00

Savage Inequalities
Jonathan Kozol
Kozol's indictment of this country's treatment of poor and nonwhite children, especially in urban areas, is stinging. After interviewing children and teachers and observing classrooms in both urban and suburban schools, Kozol concludes that our system is not only segregated but full of injustices far greater than most of us suppose. $14.00

Creative Conflict Resolution: More than 200 Activities for Keeping Peace in the Classroom
William Kreidler
Kreidler includes writing, negotiation and mediation activities, all of which help teachers deal creatively with students' anger, prejudice and aggression. It also includes a section for teachers about dealing with antagonism from parents, administrators and other teachers. $12.95

Beyond Heroes and Holidays: A Practical Guide to K-12 Antiracist , Multicultural Education and Staff Development
Edited by Enid Lee, Deborah Menkhart and Margaret Okazawa-Rey
This important resource is full of both theory and activities to help educators move beyond tokenism and simple ideas of tolerance to help children understand what it means to live in a multicultural society where racism, classism and unfair power structures are definitely not things of the past. Includes many creative discussion ideas and responses to specific prejudiced comments and behavior. $27.00

Rethinking Schools: An Agenda for Change

David Levine et al

A fascinating anthology of progressive voices in the debate over public education, this book is an offshoot of the wonderful newspaper of the same name from Milwaukee, Wisconsin. The dedicated educators who worked on this project have been the most articulate protesters against the fundamentalist agenda many people in power want to impose on our schools. Read chapters on school "choice," critical thinking about *The Lorax*, and many more controversial and interesting topics. $16.00

Lies My Teacher Told Me: Everything Your American History Book Got Wrong

James W. Loewen

Loewen has thoroughly researched the history textbooks used in most high-school classrooms in this country. Not only has he documented tremendous inaccuracies, he has exposed the insipid, mindless patriotism that characterizes most history books and puts many high-school students to sleep. Each chapter begins with information about the exciting and controversial truth of an era in this nation's history, then goes on to tell the inaccurate, boring version with which most of us are already familiar. This book is a classic, a must for every teacher and student of U.S. history. $14.00

Hands on Latin America: Art Activities for All Ages

Yvonne Merrill

This resource for teachers includes many full-color photographs of artifacts and popular folk art as well as clear instructions for each art project on the facing page. Merrill gives a good overview of Mayan, Inca, Aztec and contemporary art, and the format is absolutely beautiful. $20.00

Hands on Asia: Art Activities for All Ages
Yvonne Merrill

Merrill and illustrator Mary Simpson have created another informative and beautiful masterpiece, this time with photographs of traditional crafts from all over Asia and detailed line drawings showing the steps for the accompanying project. $20.00

Tales of the Shimmering Sky: Ten Global Folktales with Activities
Susan Milord

In an attractive, brightly colored book, Susan Milord combines retold folktales with illustrated science and hands-on activities about such natural forces as the wind, the lunar calendar and the division of day from night. A wonderful way to get kids interested in science. $15.95

Schoolgirls: Young Women, Self Esteem and the Confidence Gap
Peggy Orenstein

Orenstein followed up her work on the AAUW report with these in-depth interviews of girls from two different schools in Northern California, one a suburban white school, the other an inner-city school. She probes the way in which eighth-grade girls are changing from confident elementary school students to the high-school girls they will become, revealing the roots of teen pregnancies, poor performance in math and science courses, eating disorders and the many other problems facing adolescent girls. This book is fascinating, important and at times surprising. $14.95

The Multicultural Game Book: More than 70 Traditional Games from 30 Countries Grades 1-6
Louise Orlando

Made for teachers of elementary grades to introduce to their students, this book is made up of engaging games that require only basic supplies. They are divided into continents of origin and are introduced with supplemental social studies activities. $15.95

Kwanzaa and Me: A Teacher's Story
Vivian Paley

The multicultural classroom is here to stay, yet many teachers and administrators are still unable to articulate to themselves, much less to their students, what cultural differences really mean. Paley has done a lot of soul searching and research and has realized the kind of affirmation of culture that children of color need, in order to come through our present system with their mental and emotional health intact. $12.95

Reviving Ophelia: Saving the Selves of Adolescent Girls
Mary Pipher

Being a teenager in the present time is confusing and difficult, and there are specific reasons why girls in particular are physically and emotionally at risk. Pipher looks at the media-saturated world of popular culture and describes what is new as well as what hasn't changed despite the feminism of the last 30 years. She explains the effect our culture has on girls in their vulnerable adolescent years and offers ideas about how we as a society can help girls become confident, successful, strong women. This book is a must for parents and teachers of girls. $14.00

Real Boys: Rescuing our Sons from the Myths of Boyhood
William Pollack

The author, a psychologist, believes we as a society have grossly underestimated boys' ability to be loving, nurturing and emotional. He explains how boys show these feelings as well as how society works to repress them and give boys conflicting, damaging messages about what it means to be a man. Pollack analyzes what boys learn at home, at school, from the media and each other in this interesting, timely book. $13.95

Everyday Acts Against Racism: Raising Children in a Multicultural Society
Maureen Reddy
The author has assembled an impressive collection of essays written by parents and teachers who are educating children to be proactive forces for change in our society and to grow up confident, strong and whole as children of color in this country. The writers are a diverse group of adults, many of whom are raising multiracial families themselves. This inspiring resource can be used both in and out of the classroom. $15.95

Failing at Fairness: How Our Schools Cheat Girls
Myra and David Sadker
The Sadkers have been studying sexism in the classroom for over two decades and have come up with overwhelming evidence that girls' achievement is stifled by gender bias in schools across the country. This book not only identifies the many ways girls are overlooked and understimulated, it includes suggestions about how parents and teachers can bring about change in their schools in order to give girls the educational opportunities and guidance they deserve. $12.00

Open Minds to Equality, Second Edition
Nancy Schniedewind and Ellen Davidson
The authors have updated this classic collection of activities for classes and other groups of children. It is still full of hands-on ways to teach about equality in areas of gender, race, class, age and ability. The updated version contains an extensive resource list and is highly recommended. $40.95

Through Indian Eyes: The Native Experience in Books for Children
Doris Seale
In addition to enlightening reviews critiquing over 100 children's books, this book includes stories, poems and articles to help educators and parents gain some understanding of the Native-American

experience. Seale helps us understand that more than common sense and attempts at sensitivity are involved in understanding Indian experiences and cultures. $25.00

Why Are All the Black Kids Sitting Together in the Cafeteria?
Beverly Daniels Tatum

Tatum is a psychologist and professor, with many years' experience talking openly with students about race issues. She incorporates her reading, teaching and listening to others in helping to clarify the discussion about racial identity. This includes how we develop our thoughts and feelings about race in ourselves, our families and the society at large, how and why this society has developed racial barriers, and how we can work to challenge the racial divide and begin to heal our nation. $13.00

Roots and Wings: Affirming Culture in Early Childhood Settings
Stacey York

York has created an excellent resource to introduce or add to multi-cultural education in any early childhood program. Includes over 60 activities as well as ideas for addressing stereotypes and creating a classroom that promotes an appreciation of diversity. $24.95

People's History of the United States, Teaching Edition
Howard Zinn

An idea whose time has come, this classic book has been abridged and augmented with activities for classroom use. A large bibliography is included for each chapter. The original book is also available for $18.00 and is still a must for anyone who has not yet discovered it. $13.00

Index by Title and Author

A

A, B, C's The American Indian Way
  Richard Red Hawk, 79

A Is for Africa
  Ifeoma Onyefelu, 45

A Is for Asia
  Cynthia Chin-Lee, 88

A Is for the Americas
  Cynthia Chin-Lee and
  Terri de la Peña, 109

Aardema, Verna
  Bimwili and the Zimwi, 37
  Borreguita and the Coyote, 48
  Bringing the Rain to
  Kapiti Plain, 37
  Oh, Kojo! How Could You!, 37
  Who's in Rabbit's House?, 37

Abby
  Jeanette Caines, 112

Abner, Allison, and Linda Villarosa
  Finding Our Way: The Teen
  Girls' Survival Guide, 159

Abuela
  Arthur Dorros, 52

Abuelita's Paradise
  Carmen Santiago Nodar, 56

Ada, Alma Flor
  The Gold Coin, 48
  Mediopollito/Half Chicken, 59

Adams, Maurianne, Lee Anne Bell,
Pat Griffin
  Teaching for Diversity and Social
  Justice: A Sourcebook, 178

Adler, David
  A Picture Book of
  Anne Frank, 100

Adler, David A.
  America's Champion Swimmer:
  Gertrude Ederle, 159

Adoff, Arnold
  In for Winter, Out for Spring, 6

Adoption Is for Always
  Linda Walvoord Girard, 113

Adventures of Connie and Diego
  Maria Garcia, 53

Adventures of High John
the Conqueror
  Steve Sanfield, 28

Aekyung's Dream
  Min Paek, 90

African Beginnings
  James Haskins and
  Kathleen Benson, 41

Afro-Bets First Book About Africa
  Veronica Freeman Ellis, 39

After the Dancing Days
  Margaret Rostkowski, 138

*Ahi, Donde Bailan/
Where Fireflies Dance*
    Lucha Corpi, 60

Ahyoka and the Talking Leaves
    Peter and Connie Roop, 79

Ajmera, Maya, and
Anna Rhesa Versola
    *Children from Australia to
    Zimbabwe: A Photographic
    Journey Around the World*, 120

Ajmera, Maya, Olateju Omoludun
and Sarah Strunk
    Extraordinary Girls, 159

Akio, Terumasa
    *Me and Alves:
    A Japanese Journey*, 82

Alan and Naomi
    Myron Levoy, 102

Albert, Richard E.
    Alejandro's Gift, 171

Alejandro's Gift
    Richard E. Albert, 171

Aliki
    A Weed Is a Flower, 1

*All the Colors We Are/
Todos los Colores de Nuestra Piel*
    Katie Kissinger, ix, 108

Allegra Maud Goldman
    Edith Konecky, 150

Allen, Debbie
    Brothers of the Night, 6

Allison, Anthony
    *Hear These Voices: Youth at the
    Edge of the Millenium*, ix, 141

Alphin, Elaine Marie
    A Bear for Miguel, 48

Alvin Ailey
    Andrea Davis Pinkney, 24

*Am I Blue? Coming Out
from the Silence*
    Marion Dane Bauer, 127

Amah, The
    Laurence Yep, 96

Amazing Grace
    Mary Hoffman, 16

*Amazing Women in American History:
A Book of Answers for Kids*
    Sue Heinemann, 163

Amazon Basin
    Jan Reynolds, 124

American Association of
University Women
    *How Schools Shortchange Girls:
    The AAUW Report: A Study of
    Major Findings on Girls and
    Women*, 178

*America's Champion Swimmer:
Gertrude Ederle*
    David A. Adler, 159

Among the Volcanoes
    Omar S. Castaneda, 51

Anansi the Spider
    Gerald McDermott, 42

*Ancient Ones: The World
of the Old-Growth Douglas Fir*
    Barbara Bash, 172

Ancona, George
    Carnaval, 49

*And Then There Was One:
The Mysteries of Extinction*
    Margery Facklam, 173

Andrews, Jan
    Very Last First Time, The, 66

Angel Child, Dragon Child
    Michele Surat, 93

Angelou, Maya
    Kofi and His Magic, 37

Angel's Kite/ La Estrella de Angel
    Alberto Blanco, 60

Annie and the Old One
    Miska Miles,

Annie on My Mind
    Nancy Garden, 128

Anzaldua, Gloria
    Friends from the Other Side, 49
    Prietita and the Ghost Woman/
    Prietita y la Llorona, 59

April and the Dragon Lady
    Lensey Namioka, 90

Arctic Memories
    Normee Ekoomiak, 71

Argueta, Manlio
    Magic Dogs of the Volcanoes/
    Los Perros Magicos de los
    Volcanes, 59

Armstrong, Jennifer
    Steal Away, 6

Arrow Over the Door
    Joseph Bruchac, 67

Ashanti to Zulu
    Margaret Musgrove, 44

Asha's Mums
    Rosamund Elwin and
    Michele Paulse, 127

At the Beach
    Huy Voun Lee, 88

At the Crossroads
    Rachel Isadora, 41

Ata, Te
    Baby Rattlesnake, 66

Atariba and Niguyona
    Harriet Rohmer, 65

Atkin, S. Beth
    Voices from the Street: Former
    Gang Members Tell Their Stories,
    141

Aunt Harriet's Underground Railroad
in the Sky
    Faith Ringgold, 26

Autobiography of Malcolm X, The
    Malcolm X, 5

Ayers, William, Jean Ann Hunt,
Therese Quinn
    Teaching for Social Justice:
    A Democracy and Education
    Reader, 178

B

Baby Rattlesnake
    Te Ata, 66

Bacharach, Susan D.
    Tell Them We Remember:
    The Story of the Holocaust, 100

Ballot Box Battle
    Emily Arnold McCully, 151

Barefoot Book of Heroic Children
    Rebecca Hazell, 134

Barefoot Book of Tropical Tales, The
    Raouf Mama, 123

Barnwell, Ysaye M.
    No Mirrors in
    My Nana's House, 7

Baseball Saved Us
    Ken Mochizuki, 137

Bash, Barbara
  *Ancient Ones: The World of the
  Old-Growth Douglas Fir,* 172
  *Desert Giant: The World of the
  Saguaro Cactus,* 172
  *In the Heart of the Village:
  The World of the
  Indian Banyan Tree,* 171
  *Shadows of the Night:
  The Hidden World of the Little
  Brown Bat,* 172
  *Tree of Life: The World of the
  African Baobab,* 172

Bass, Ellen, and Kate Kaufman
  *Free Your Mind: The Book for Gay,
  Lesbian and Bisexual Youth and
  Their Families,* 127

Bauer, Marion Dane
  *Am I Blue? Coming Out from
  the Silence,* 127

Bayless, Maureen
  Strike, 131

Baylor, Byrd
  When Clay Sings, 66

Bean Trees, The
  Barbara Kingsolver, 150

Bear for Miguel, A
  Elaine Marie Alphin, 48

Beatty, Patricia
  Lupita Mañana, 49

Begay, Shonto
  *Navajo: Visions and Voices Across
  the Mesa,* 66

Berclaw, Edna Coe
  Halmoni's Day, 82

Bernhard, Emery and
Durga Bernhard
  *A Ride on Mother's Back: A Day of
  Baby Carrying Around the World,*
  120

Best Bad Thing, The
  Yoshiko Uchida, 94

*Between Earth and Sky: Legends of
Native-American Sacred Places*
  Joseph Bruchac, 67

Between Madison and Palmetto
  Jacqueline Woodson, 33

*Beyond Heroes and Holidays:
A Practical Guide to K-12 Antiracist,
Multicultural Education and Staff
Development*
  Enid Lee, Deborah Menkhart
  and Margaret Okazawa-Rey,
  ed., 182

Beyond Safe Boundaries
  Margaret Sacks, 46

Beyond the Ridge
  Paul Goble, 73

Bial, Raymond
  The Underground Railroad, 1

Bicycle Rider
  Mary Sciosca, 28

Big Book for Peace
  Ann Durell, ed., 133

Bimwili and the Zimwi
  Verna Aardema, 37

Birchbark House, The
  Louise Erdrich, 71

*Bird Who Cleans the World and Other
Mayan Fables, The*
  Victor Montejo, 56

*Birthdays: Celebrating Life Around
the World*
  Eve B. Feldman, 120

*Black Americans:
A History in Their Own Words*
  Milton Meltzer, 4

Black and Red: Portraits of Independent Spirits
 Morgan Monceaux and Ruth Katcher, 4

Black Snowman, The
 Phil Mendez, 22

Blanco, Alberto
 Angel's Kite/ La Estrella de Angel, 60

Block, Francesca Lia
 Dangerous Angels, 146
 Girl Goddess #9, 146

Blomquist, Geraldine
 Zachary's New Home: A Story for Foster and Adopted Children, 112

Blood, Peter
 Rise Up Singing, 179

Bobbin Girl, The
 Emily Arnold McCully, 151

Bode, Jane
 New Kids in Town: Oral Histories of Immigrant Teens, 106

Bonjour, Lonnie
 Faith Ringgold, 26

Book of Black Heroes from A to Z
 Wade Hudson, 3

Book of Black Heroes Volume II: Great Women in the Struggle
 Toyomi Igus, 3

Borreguita and the Coyote
 Verna Aardema, 48

Bound for America: The Forced Migration of Africans to the New World
 James Haskins and Kathleen Benson, 2

Boundless Grace
 Mary Hoffman, 16

Boy Becomes a Man at Wounded Knee, A
 Ted Wood, with Wanbli Numba Afraid of Hawk, 81

Boyd, Candy Dawson
 Forever Friends, 7
 Charlie Pippin, 131

Boys Will Be Men: Raising Our Sons for Courage, Caring and Commitment
 Paul Kivel, 181

Bracelet, The
 Yoshiko Uchida, 140

Brave New Girls: Creative Ideas to Help Girls Be Confident, Healthy, and Happy
 Jeanette Gadeberg, 161

Bread, Bread, Bread
 Ann Morris and Ken Heyman, 124

Breckler, Rosemary
 Sweet Dried Apples: A Vietnamese Wartime Childhood, 131

Brenner, Barbara
 Wagon Wheels, 7

Bridges, Ruby
 Through My Eyes, 1

Bright Eyes, Brown Skin
 Cheryl Willis Hudson, 17

Brill, Marlene Targ
 Journey for Peace: The Story of Rigoberta Manchu, 49

Bringing the Rain to Kapiti Plain
 Verna Aardema, 37

Brodzinsky, Anne Braff
 The Mulberry Bird, 112

Brothers of the Night
 Debbie Allen, 6

Brown Angels
 Walter Dean Myers, 23

Brown, Tricia
  *Children of the Midnight Sun:
  Young Native Voices of Alaska*, 67

Bruchac, Joseph
  Arrow Over the Door, 67
  *Between Earth and Sky: Legends
  of Native-American Sacred Places*,
  67
  Children of the Longhouse, 68
  *The Earth Under Sky
  Bear's Feet*, 69
  The First Strawberries, ix, 68
  *Great Ball Game:
  A Muskogee Story*, 69
  Native-American Stories, 69
  *Native-American Animal
  Stories*, 69
  Return of the Sun, 69
  The Story of the Milky Way, 69
  *Thirteen Moons on a
  Turtle's Back*, 69
  The Trail of Tears, 70

Bruchac, Joseph, and
Michael J. Caduto
  *Keepers of the Animals:
  Native-American Stories and
  Wildlife Activities for Children*,
  179
  *Keepers of the Earth:
  Native-American Stories with
  Environmental Activities for
  Children*, 179
  *Keepers of Life: Discovering Plants
  Through Native-American
  Stories and Earth Activities for
  Children*, 179
  *Keepers of the Night:
  Native-American Stories and
  Nocturnal Activities for Children*,
  179

Bryan, Ashley
  *The Night Has Ears:
  African Proverbs*, 38

Bud, Not Buddy
  Christopher Paul Curtis, ix, 11

Buddha
  Demi, 83

Buettner, Dan
  *Sovietrek: A Journey by Bicycle
  Across Russia*, 98

Buffalo Woman
  Paul Goble, 73

Bunting, Eve
  Fly Away Home, 142
  Going Home, 50
  Smoky Night, 142
  So Far from the Sea, 132

Burchignani, Walter
  Tell No One Who You Are, 100

Burden-Patman, Denise
  Imani's Gift at Kwanzaa, 7

Buss, Fran Leper, with
Daisy Cubias
  Journey of the Sparrows, 50

Butler, Jerry
  *A Drawing in the Sand:
  The Story of African-American
  Art*, ix, 8

C

Caines, Jeanette
  Abby, 112

Calendar of Festivals, A
  Cherry Gilchrist, 121

*Calle Es Libre, La/
The Streets Are Free*
  Karusa, 62

*Calling the Doves/
El Canto de las Palomas*
  Juan Felipe Herrera, 61

Cameron, Ann
  Julian's Glorious Summer, 8
  Stories Huey Tells, 9
  Stories Julian Tells, 8
  More Stories Julian Tells, 8
  *The Most Beautiful Place
  in the World,* 50

Cannon, Janell
  Stellaluna, 172

Cano, Robin B.
  *Lucita Comes Home to
  Oaxaca/Lucita Regresa a Oaxaca,*
  60

*Canto de las Palomas, El/
Calling the Doves*
  Juan Filipe Herrera, 61

Carlsson-Paige, Nancy, and
Diane Levin
  *Who's Calling the Shots? How to
  Respond Effectively to Kids'
  Fascination with War Play and
  War Toys,* 180

Carnaval
  George Ancona, 49

Carnes, Jim
  *Us and Them: A History of
  Intolerance in America,* 142

Carrying
  Gwenyth Swain, 126

Castaneda, Omar S.
  Among the Volcanos, 51

Catherine Called Birdy
  Karen Cushman, 147

*Celebrate! In Southeast Asia
Celebrate! In South Asia*
  Joe Viesti and Diane Hall, 94

Celebrating
  Gwenyth Swain, 126

Celebrating Families
  Rosemarie Hausherr, 117

Cha, Dia
  *Dia's Story Cloth: The Hmong
  People's Journey of Freedom,* 82

Chafe, William H.
  *Young Oxford History of Women
  in the United States. 10 The Road
  to Equality: 1962-Present,* 167

Chain of Fire
  Beverly Naidoo, 44

Chambers, Veronica
  *Marisol and Magdelena: The
  Sound of our Sisterhood,* 51

Charlie Pippin
  Candy Dawson Boyd, 131

Checking on the Moon
  Jenny Davis, 143

Cherry, Lynne
  The Great Kapok Tree, 173
  A River Ran Wild, 173

Chicken Sunday
  Patricia Polacco, 109

*Chidi Only Likes Blue: An African
Book of Colors*
  Ifeoma Onyefulu, 46

Child of the Owl
  Laurence Yep, 96

*Children from Australia to Zimbabwe:
A Photographic Journey Around the
World*
  Maya Ajmera and
  Anna Rhesa Versola, 120

Children in China
  Michael Karhausen, 87

Children Just Like Me
  Barnabas and Anabel
  Kindersley, in association with
  UNICEF, ix, 122

Children Just Like Me: Celebrations
Barnabas and Anabel
Kindersley,   122

Children Just Like Me:
Our Favorite Stories
Jamila Gavin,   122

Children of Guatemala
Jules Hermes,   54

Children of India
Jules Hermes,   86

Children of Mauritania: Days in the
Desert and by the River Shore
Lauren Goodsmith,   40

Children of Morocco
Jules Hermes,   41

Children of the Longhouse
Joseph Bruchac,   68

Children of the Midnight Sun:
Young Native Voices of Alaska
Tricia Brown,   67

Children of the Morning Light:
Wampanoag Tales
Manitonquat, (Told by),   76

Children of the River
Linda Crew,   83

Chin, Charlie
China's Bravest Girl,   83

Chin-Lee, Cynthia
A Is for Asia,   88

Chin-Lee, Cynthia, and
Terri de la Peña
A Is for the Americas,   109

China's Bravest Girl
Charlie Chin,   83

Chinese New Year's Dragon
Rachel Sing,   92

Chipmunk Song
Joanne Ryder,   176

Ciment, James
Scholastic Encyclopedia of the
North American Indian,   70

Circuit, The: Stories from the Life of a
Migrant Child
Francisco Jimenez,   55

Clay Marble, The
Mingfong Ho,   135

Close-Up
Szabinka Dudevszky,   143

Coconut Kind of Day
Lynn Joseph,   35

Coerr, Eleanor
Meiko and the Fifth Treasure,   132
Sadako,   132
Sadako and the
Thousand Paper Cranes,   132

Cohen, Barbara
Make a Wish, Molly,   100
Molly's Pilgrim,   101
Thank You, Jackie Robinson,   101

Cohn, Janice
Why Did It Happen? Helping
Children Cope in a Violent World,
143

Cole, Babette
Prince Cinders,   168
Princess Smartypants,   147

Coleman, Evelyn
To Be a Drum,   9
White Socks Only,   9

Collicott, Sharleen
Toestomper and the
Caterpillars,   168

Colman, Penny
Girls: A History of Growing Up
Female in America,   160

Colon, Raul
Tomàs and the Library Lady,   51

Colors of Us, The
    Karen Katz, 108

Come Back, Salmon
    Molly Cone, 173

Come On, Rain!
    Karen Hesse, 107

Coming Home: From the Life of Langston Hughes
    Floyd Cooper, 10

Coming of Age in America: A Multicultural Anthology
    Mary Frosch, ed., 107

Coming of Age in Mississippi
    Anne Moody, 5

Con Mi Hermano/With My Brother
    Eileen Roe, 65

Cone, Molly
    Come Back, Salmon, 173

Cooke, Trish
    So Much, 9

Cool Women: The Thinking Girl's Guide to the Hippest Women in the World
    Pam Nelson, 165

Cooney, Barbara
    Eleanor, 147

Cooper, Floyd
    Coming Home: From the Life of Langston Hughes, 10
    Mandela, 38

Cornrows
    Camille Yarbrough, 34

Corpi, Lucha
    Where Fireflies Dance/Ahi Donde Bailan los Luciernagas, 60

Counting to Tar Beach
    Faith Ringgold, 26

Cowen-Fletcher, Jane
    It Takes a Village, 38

Cowley, Joy
    Gràcias the Thanksgiving Turkey, 51

Creative Confllict Resolution: More Than 200 Activities for Keeping Peace in the Classroom
    William Kreidler, 182

Crew, Linda
    Children of the River, 83

Crossing the Starlight Bridge
    Alice Mead, 77

Crow Chief
    Paul Goble, 73

Cuadros de la Familia
    Carmen Lomas Garza, 61

Cuba: After the Revolution
    Bernard Wolf, 58

Cuento de Ferdinando, El
    Munro Leaf, 62

Curry, Barbara, and James Michael Brody
    Sweet Words So Brave: The Story of African-American Literature, 10

Curtis, Christopher Paul
    Bud, Not Buddy, ix, 11
    The Watsons Go to Birmingham—1963, ix, 10

Curtis, Jamie Lee
    Tell Me Again About the Night I Was Born, 113

Cushman, Karen
    Catherine Called Birdy, 147
    The Midwife's Apprentice, 148

Cut from the Same Cloth
    Robert San Souci, 154

D

D is for Doufu: An Alphabet Book of Chinese Culture
Maywan Shen Krach, 87

Daddy's Roommate
Michael Willhoite, 130

Daldry, Jeremy
The Teenage Guy's Survival Guide: The Real Deal on Girls, Growing Up and Other Guy Stuff, 169

Dangerous Angels
Francesca Lia Block, 146

Dark-Thirty, The
Patricia McKissack, 21

Dat's New Year
Linda Smith, 106

Dave at Night
Gail Carson Levine, 109

Davidson, Sue
Getting the Real Story: Nellie Bly and Ida B. Wells, 160
A Heart in Politics: Jeanette Rankin and Patsy Mink, 160

Davis, Jenny
Checking on the Moon, 143

Day, Marie
The Dragon in the Rocks, 148

Day Gogo Went to Vote, The
Eleanor Batezat Sisulu, 46

Day of Ahmed's Secret, The
Florence Parry Heide, 104

Deal with It!
A Whole New Approach to Your Body, Brain and Life as a Gurl
Esther Drill, ix, 161

Dear Mrs. Parks: A Dialogue with Today's Youth
Rosa Parks, 101

Dear One, The
Jacqueline Woodson, 34

Death of the Iron Horse
Paul Goble, 73

Demi
Buddha, 83
Happy New Year, 83
One Grain of Rice: A Mathematical Folktale, 84

Demos, John
Young Oxford History of Women in the United States. 1 The Tried and the True: Native-American Women Confronting Colonization, 166

DePaola, Tomie
Oliver Button Is a Sissy, ix, 169

Desert Giant: The World of the Saguaro Cactus
Barbara Bash, 172

Deshpande, Chris
Diwali, 106

DeSpain, Pleasant
Thirty-Three Multicultural Tales to Tell, 180

Deutsch, Sarah Jane
Young Oxford History of Women in the United States. 8 From Ballots to Breadlines: 1920-1961, 167

Devil in Vienna, The
Doris Orgel, 103

Devil's Arithmetic, The
Jane Yolen, 103

Dia's Story Cloth: The Hmong People's Journey of Freedom
Dia Cha, 82

Diaz, Jorge Ancona
    *Pablo Recuerda la Fiesta del Dia
    de los Muertos*, 60

*Did You Hear the Wind Sing Your
Name? An Oneida Song of Spring*
    Sandra De Coteau Orie, 78

Dinner at Aunt Connie's House
    Faith Ringgold, 26

DiSalvo-Ryan, Dyanne
    *Uncle Willie and the
    Soup Kitchen*, 143

Diwali
    Chris Deshpande, 106

*Do I Have a Daddy? A Story About a
Single Parent Child*
    Jeanne Warren Lindsay, 118

Dolphin, Laurie
    Our Journey from Tibet, 84

Don't Bet on the Prince
    Jack Zipes, 158

Dorris, Michael
    Morning Girl, 71

Dorros, Arthur
    Abuela, 52
    Radio Man, 60
    Tonight Is Carnival, 52

Down Home at Miss Dessa's
    Bettye Stroud, 29

Down in the Piney Woods
    Ethel Footman Smothers, 28

Down Under
    Jan Reynolds, 124

Dragon in the Rocks, The
    Marie Day, 148

Dragon Kite of the Autumn Moon
    Valerie Reddix , 90

*Dragon Lover, The, and Other Chinese
Proverbs*
    Yong-Sheng Xuan, 95

Dragon Soup
    Arlene Williams, 157

Dragonwings
    Laurence Yep, ix, 97

*Drawing in the Sand, A: The Story of
African-American Art*
    Jerry Butler, 8

Dream Keeper, The, and Other Poems
    Langston Hughes, 18

Drill, Esther
    *Deal with It! A Whole New
    Approach to Your Body, Brain
    and Life as a Gurl*, 161

Dudevszky, Szabinka
    Close-Up, 143

Duncan, Alice Faye
    *The National Civil Rights Museum
    Celebrates Everyday People*, 2

Durell, Ann, ed.
    Big Book for Peace, 133

Dust from Old Bones
    Sandra Forrester , 12

E

Ear, the Eye and the Arm, The
    Nancy Farmer, 39

Earth Under Sky Bear's Feet, The
    Joseph Bruchac, 69

Eating
    Gwenyth Swain, 126

Eco-Women: Protectors of the Earth
    Willow Ann Sirch, 177

Eid-Ul-Fur
    Susheila Stone, 107

Ekoomiak, Normee
Arctic Memories, 71

Eleanor
Barbara Cooney, 147

Eleanor Roosevelt: A Life of Discovery
Russell Friedman, 161

Elinda Who Danced in the Sky:
An Estonian Folktale
Lynn Moroney, 98

Ellis, Veronica Freeman
Afro-Bets First Book
About Africa, 39
Land of the Four Winds, 38

Elwin, Rosamund, and
Michele Paulse
Asha's Mums, 127

Emeka's Gift: An African
Counting Story
Ifeoma Onyefulu, 46

En Mi Familia/In My Family
Carmen Lomas Garza, 61

Erdrich, Louise
The Birchbark House, 71

Erlbach, Arlene
The Families Book: True Stories
About Real Kids and the People
They Live With, 117

Esbensen, Barbara Juster
The Star Maiden, 71

Escape from Slavery: The Boyhood of
Frederick Douglass in His Own Words
Michael McCurdy, ed.
and illus., 4

Estrella de Angel, La /Angel's Kite
Alberto Blanco, 60

Everyday Acts Against Racism:
Raising Children
in a Multicultural Society
Maureen Reddy, 186

Everygirl's Guide to Feminism
Kate Hughes, 163

Extraordinary Girls
Maya Ajmera, Olateju
Omoludun and Sarah Strunk,
159

F

Facklam, Margery
And Then There Was One:
The Mysteries of Extinction, 173

Failing at Fairness: How Our Schools
Cheat Girls
Myra and David Sadker, 186

Fairy Tale Collections Featuring
Strong Women and Girls
Don't Bet on the Prince
Jack Zipes, 158
Maid of the North
Ethel Phelps, 157
Tatterhood and Other Tales
Ethel Phelps, 158

Faithful Friend, The
Robert San Souci, 36

Families
Ann Morris, 119

Families
Ann Morris
and Ken Heyman, 123

Families
Meredith Tax, 119

Families: A Celebration of Diversity,
Commitment and Love
Aylette Jenness, 118

Families Are Different
Nina Pellegrini, 119

Families Book, The: True Stories
About Real Kids and the People they
Live With
Arlene Erlbach, 117

Families: Poems Celebrating the
African-American Experience
    Dorothy and Michael
    Strickland, illus., 28

Family Pictures/
Cuadros de la Familia
    Carmen Lomas Garza, 61

Far North
    Jan Reynolds, 124

Farmer, Nancy
    The Ear, the Eye, and the Arm, 39
    A Girl Named Disaster, ix, 39

Fearless Girls, Wise Women, and
Beloved Sisters: Heroines in Folktales
from Around the World
    Kathleen Ragan, 154

Feelings, Muriel
    Jambo Means Hello, 40
    Moja Means One, 40
    Zamani Goes to Market, 40

Feelings, Tom, illus.
    Soul Looks Back in Wonder, ix, 11

Feldman, Eve B.
    Birthdays: Celebrating Life Around
    the World, 120

Felita
    Nicholasa Mohr, 55

Fernando's Gift/El Regalo de Fernando
    Douglas Keister, 175

Fiesta!
    Ginger Fogelsong Guy, 54

Finding Our Way: The Teen Girls'
Survival Guide
    Allison Abner and Linda
    Villarosa, 159

Fine, Edith Hope
    Under the Lemon Moon, ix, 52

Finkelstein, Norman
    Remember Not to Forget, 101

Fire at the Triangle Factory
    Holly Littlefield, 144

First Apple
    Ching Young Russell, 91

First Strawberries, The
    Joseph Bruchac, ix, 68

Flecha Al Sol
    Gerald McDermott, 63

Fleischner, Jennifer
    I Was Born a Slave: The Story of
    Harriet Jacobs, 2

Fly Away Home
    Eve Bunting, 142

Follow in Their Footsteps: Biographies
of Ten Outstanding African Americans
    Glenette Tilley Turner, 5

Forbidden Talent
    Redwing T. Nez, 78

Ford, Michael Thomas
    OutSpoken: Role Models from the
    Lesbian and Gay Community, 127

Forest Wife, The
    Theresa Tomlinson, 156

Forever Friends
    Candy Dawson Boyd, 7

Forrester, Sandra
    Dust from Old Bones, 12

Franklin, Kristin, and
Nancy McGirr
    Out of the Dump, 53

Franklin, Robert Leslie
    In the Shadow of a Rainbow, 72

Frasier, Debra
    On the Day You Were Born,
    ix, 173

Frederick Douglass:
The Last Day of Slavery
    William Miller, 4

Free Your Mind:
The Book for Gay, Lesbian and
Bisexual Youth and Their Families
  Ellen Bass and
  Kate Kaufman, 127

Freedom Songs
  Yvette Moore, 22

Freedom's Fruit
  William Hooks, 16

Freedom's Gifts:
A Juneteenth Story
  Valerie Wesley, 32

Fricke, Aaron
  Reflections of a Rock Lobster, 128

Friedman, Ina
  How My Parents Learned to Eat,
  84

Friedman, Russell
  Eleanor Roosevelt:
  A Life of Discovery, 161

Friends from the Other Side
  Gloria Anzaldua, 49

From Abenaki to Zuni: A Dictionary of
Native-American Tribes
  Evelyn Wolfson, 81

From the Notebooks of Melanin Sun
  Jacqueline Woodson, 33

Front Porch Stories
at the One-Room School
  Eleanora Tate, 29

Frosch, Mary, ed.
  Coming of Age in America:
  A Multicultural Anthology, 107

Frozen North
  Jan Reynolds, 125

Furlong, Monica
  Juniper, 148
  Wise Child, 148

G

Gadeberg, Jeanette
  Brave New Girls: Creative Ideas to
  Help Girls Be Confident, Healthy
  and Happy, 161

Galimoto
  Karen Lynn Williams, 47

Gallo, Donald
  Join In: Multiethnic Short Stories
  by Outstanding Writers for
  Young Adults, 107

Garay, Luis
  The Long Road, 53

Garcia, Maria
  Adventures of Connie and Diego,
  53

Garden, Nancy
  Annie on My Mind, 128

Gardener, The
  Sarah Stewart, 156

Gardner-Loulan, JoAnn
  Period, 162

Garland, Sherry
  The Lotus Seed, 85
  Song of the Buffalo Boy, 133

Garza, Carmen Lomas
  Family Pictures/
  Cuadros de la Familia, 61
  In my Family/En mi Familia, 61

Gaskins, Pearl Fuyo
  What Are You? Voices of Mixed-
  Race Young People, 107

Gavin, Jamila
  Children Just Like Me:
  Our Favorite Stories, 122

George, Jean
  Julie of the Wolves, 72
  Talking Earth, 72

Georgia O'Keefe
  Robyn Montana Turner, 166

Geraghty, Paul
  The Hunter, 40

Geraldine
  The Goat in the Rug, 72

Gerstein, Mordecai
  The Mountains of Tibet, 85

Getting the Real Story:
Nellie Bly and Ida B. Wells
  Sue Davidson, 160

Ghazi, Suhaib Hamid
  Ramadan, 104

Gift for Abuelita, A: Celebrating the
Day of the Dead
  Nancy Luenn, 62

Gift Giver, The
  Joyce Hansen, 14

Gift Horse
  S. D. Nelson, 77

Gift of the Sacred Dog, The
  Paul Goble, 73

Girard, Linda Walvoord
  Adoption Is for Always, 113
  We Adopted You, Benjamin Koo,
  113

Girl Who Loved Wild Horses, The
  Paul Goble, 73

Girl Goddess #9
  Francesca Lia Block, 146

Gilchrist, Cherry
  A Calendar of Festivals, 121
  Stories from the Silk Road, 85

Gillespie, Peggy, ed.
  Love Makes a Family: Portraits of
  Lesbian, Gay, Bisexual and
  Transgender Parents and Their
  Families, 117
  Of Many Colors: Portraits of
  Multiracial Families, 180

Gilmore, Rachna
  Lights for Gita, 86
  Roses for Gita, 85

Girl Named Disaster, A
  Nancy Farmer, ix, 39

Girls: A History of Growing Up Female
in America
  Penny Colman, 160

Girls Think of Everything: Stories of
Inventions by Women
  Catherine Thimmesh, 166

Girls to the Rescue Series
  Bruce Lansky, ed., 150

Giving Thanks: A Native American
Good Morning Message
  Chief Jake Swamp, 80

Goat in the Rug, The
  Geraldine (aka Charles Blood),
  72

Goble, Paul
  Beyond the Ridge, 73
  Buffalo Woman, 73
  Crow Chief, 73
  Death of the Iron Horse, 73
  The Gift of the Sacred Dog, 73
  The Girl Who
  Loved Wild Horses, 73
  The Great Race, 73
  The Lost Children, 74
  Red Hawk's Account of
  Custer's Last Battle, 74
  Remaking the Earth, 74

Going Home
  Eve Bunting, 50

Going Home
  Nicholasa Mohr, 56

Gold Coin, The
  Alma Flor Ada, 48

*Golden Flower, The: A Taino Myth
from Puerto Rico*
  Nina Jaffe, 55

Goldberg, Michael
  *Young Oxford History of Women
  in the United States. 4 Breaking
  New Ground: 1800-1848*, 167

Goodsmith, Lauren
  *Children of Muritania: Days in
  the Desert and by the River Shore*,
  40

Gordon, Sheila
  Waiting for the Rain, 41

Grab Hands and Run
  Francis Temple, 57

Gracias the Thanksgiving Turkey
  Joy Cowley, 51

Grandchildren of the Incas
  Matti Pitkanen, 78

Grandfather's Dream
  Holly Keller, 87

Grandmama's Joy
  Eloise Greenfield, 12

Gray, Heather M.,
and Samantha Phillips
  *Real Girl, Real World: Tools for
  Finding Your True Self*, ix, 162

Great Ball Game: A Muskogee Story
  Joseph Bruchac, 69

Great Kapok Tree, The
  Lynne Cherry, 173

Great Migration, The
  Jacob Lawrence, 20

Great Race, The
  Paul Goble, 72

Greenfield, Eloise
  Grandmama's Joy, 12
  Night on Neighborhood Street, 12

Greenwood, Barbara
  *The Last Safe House: A Story of
  the Underground Railroad*, 13

Grossman, Patricia
  The Saturday Market, 53

*Growing Up Gay:
A Literary Anthology*
  Bennett Singer, ed., 130

Growing Up: It's a Girl Thing
  Mavis Jukes, 163

Guatemalan Family
  Michael Malone, 108

Guthrie, Woody
  This Land Is Your Land, 133

Guy, Ginger Fogelsong
  Fiesta!, 54

H

Haag, Pamela
  *Voices of a Generation:
  Teenage Girls Report About Their
  Lives Today*, 181

*Habari Gani? What's the News?
A Kwanzaa Story*
  Sundaira Morninghouse, 23

Habibi
  Naomi Shihab Nye, 137

Hale, Sarah Josepha
  Mary Had a Little Lamb, 13

Half-Chicken/Mediopollito
  Alma Flor Ada, 59

Halmoni's Day
  Edna Coe Berclaw, 82

Hamanaka, Sheila
  I Look Like a Girl, 149
  *The Journey: Japanese Americans,
  Racism and Renewal*, 133

Hamilton, Virginia
  *Her Stories: Folktales, Fairy Tales
  and True Tales*, 13
  *In the Beginning: Creation Stories
  from Around the World*, 121
  Jaguarundi, 174
  *Many Thousand Gone:
  African Americans from Slavery
  to Freedom*, 14
  The People Could Fly, 14
  Sweet Whispers, Brother Rush, 14
  *When Birds Could Talk and
  Bats Could Sing*, 13

Handful of Seeds, A
  Monica Hughes, 54

*Hands on Asia: Art Activities
for All Ages*
  Yvonne Merrill, 184

*Hands on Latin America:
Art Activities for All Ages*
  Yvonne Merrill, 183

Hannigan, Lynne
  Sam's Passover, 106

Hansen, Joyce
  The Gift Giver, 14
  The Heart Calls Home, 15
  Out from This Place, 15
  Which Way Freedom?, 15
  *Women of Hope: African
  Americans Who Made a
  Difference*, 162

Happy Adoption Day!
  John McCutcheon, 115

Happy Birthday, Martin Luther King
  Jean Marzollo, 20

Happy New Year!
  Demi, 83

Happy to Be Nappy
  bell hooks, 16

Harlem
  Walter Dean Myers, 23

Hart, Philip
  *Up in the Air: The Story of
  Bessie Coleman*, 162

*Harvest Birds The/
Los Pajaros De La Cosecha*
  Blanca Lopez de Mariscal, 62

Haskins, Francine
  I Remember "121", 15

Haskins, James,
and Kathleen Benson
  African Beginnings, 41
  *Bound for America: The Forced
  Migration of Africans to the New
  World*, 2

Hats, Hats, Hats
  Ann Morris
  and Ken Heyman, 123

Hausherr, Rosemarie
  Celebrating Families, 117

Have a Happy...
  Mildred Pitts Walter, 31

Haveli
  Suzanne Fisher Staples, 155

Hazell, Rebecca
  Barefoot Book of Heroic Children,
  134

Hazen-Hammond, Susan
  *Thunder Bear and Ko: The Buffalo
  Nation and Nambe Pueblo*, 74

*Hear These Voices: Youth at the Edge
of the Millennium*
  Anthony Allison, ix, 141

*Hearing Us Out: Voices from the
Lesbian and Gay Community*
  Roger Sutton, 130

Hearne, Betsy
  Seven Brave Women, 149

Heart Calls Home, The
  Joyce Hanson, 15

Heart in Politics, A: Jeanette Rankin and Patsy Mink
  Sue Davidson, 160

Heather Has Two Mommies
  Leslea Newman, 129

Heetunka's Harvest: A Tale of the Plains Indians
  Jennifer Berry Jones, 75

Heide, Florence Parry
  The Day of Ahmed's Secret, 104

Heide, Florence Parry, and Judith Heide Gilliland
  House of Wisdom, 104
  Sami and the Time of the Troubles, 134

Heinemann, Sue
  Amazing Women in American History: A Book of Answers for Kids, 163

Her Stories: Folktales, Fairy Tales and True Tales
  Virginia Hamilton, 13

Hermes, Jules
  Children of Guatemala, 54
  Children of India, 86
  Children of Morocco, 41

Heron, Ann
  Two Teenagers in Twenty: Writing by Gay and Lesbian Youth, 128

Heron, Ann, and Meredith Maran
  How Would You Feel If Your Dad Was Gay?, 128

Herrera, Juan Felipe
  Calling the Doves/ El Canto de las Palomas, 61
  The Upside Down Boy/ El Nino de Cabeza, 61

Hesse, Karen
  Come On, Rain!, 107
  Letters from Rifka, 101
  Phoenix Rising, 174
  A Time of Angels, 134

Hide and Sneak
  Michael Avaarluk Kusugak, 75

Himalaya
  Jan Reynolds, 125

Historia de Los Colores, La/ The Story of the Colors
  Subcomandante Marcos, 63

Ho, Mingfong
  The Clay Marble, 135
  Hush, 86

Hoffman, Mary
  Amazing Grace, 16
  Boundless Grace, 16

Hold Fast to Dreams
  Andrea Pinkney, 25

Hollyer, Beatrice
  Wake Up, World: A Day in the Life of Children Around the World, 121

Home to Medicine Mountain
  Chiori Santiago, 79

Homeless
  Bernard Wolf, 145

hooks, bell
  Happy to Be Nappy, 16

Hooks, William
  Freedom's Fruit, 16

Hopkinson, Deborah
  Maria's Comet, 149
  *Sweet Clara and the
  Freedom Quilt*, 17

Horace
  Holly Keller, 114

House of Wisdom
  Florence Parry Heide and
  Judith Heide Gilliland, 104

Houses and Homes
  Ann Morris and
  Ken Heyman, 123

*Houses of Bark: Tipi, Wigwam and
Longhouse—The Woodland Indians*
  Bonnie Shemie, 80

*Houses of Hide and Earth—
Plains Indians*
  Bonnie Shemie, 80

*Houses of Snow, Skin and Bones—
The Far North*
  Bonnie Shemie, 80

Houses of Wood—The Northwest Coast
  Bonnie Shemie, 80

How It Feels to Be Adopted
  Jill Krementz, 115

How My Parents Learned to Eat
  Ina Friedman, 84

*How Schools Shortchange Girls:
The AAUW Report: A Study of Major
Findings on Girls and Education*
  American Association of
  University Women, 178

How the Forest Grew
  William Jaspersohn, 174

*How Would You Feel If Your Dad
Was Gay?*
  Ann Heron and
  Meredith Maran, 128

Howlett, Bud
  I'm New Here, 54

Hoyt-Goldsmith, Diane
  Pueblo Storyteller, 75

Hubbard, Jim
  *Lives Turned Upside Down:
  Homeless Children in their Own
  Words and Photographs*, 144

Hudson, Cheryl Willis
  Bright Eyes, Brown Skin, 17
  *In Praise of Our Fathers and
  Mothers: A Black Family
  Treasury by Outstanding Authors
  and Artists*, 17

Hudson, Wade
  *Book of Black Heroes
  from A to Z*, 3
  *Pass It On: African-American
  Poetry for Children*, 17
  *In Praise of Our Fathers and
  Mothers: A Black Family
  Treasury by Outstanding Authors
  and Artists*, 17

Hughes, Kate
  Everygirl's Guide to Feminism,
  163

Hughes, Langston
  *The Dream Keeper and
  Other Poems*, 18

Hughes, Monica
  A Handful of Seeds, 54

The Hunter
  Paul Geraghty, 40

Hush
  Mingfong Ho, 86

Hyppolite, Joanne
  Seth and Samona, 18

I

*I Am an American: The True Story of
Japanese Internment*
  Jerry Stanley, 139

I Have a Dream
Dr. Martin Luther King, Jr., 19

I Look Like a Girl
Sheila Hamanaka, 149

I Love My Hair!
Natasha Anastasia Tarpley, 29

I Remember "121"
Francine Haskins, 15

I See the Rhythm
Toyomi Igus, 18

I Was Born a Slave: The Story of Harriet Jacobs
Jennifer Fleischner, 2

If a Bus Could Talk: The Story of Rosa Parks
Faith Ringgold, 27

Igus, Toyomi
Books of Black Heroes Volume II: Great Women in the Struggle, 3
I See the Rhythm, 18

I'm New Here
Bud Howlett, 54

Imani's Gift at Kwanzaa
Denise Burden-Patman, 7

In for Winter, Out for Spring
Arnold Adoff, 6

In My Family/ En Mi Familia
Carmen Lomas Garza, 61

In Praise of Our Fathers and Mothers: A Black Family Treasury by Outstanding Authors and Artists
Wade Hudson and Cheryl Willis Hudson, eds., 17

In the Beginning: Creation Stories from Around the World
Virginia Hamilton, 121

In the Heart of the Village: The World of the Indian Banyan Tree
Barbara Bash, 171

In the Park
Huy Voun Lee, 88

In the Rainfield: Who Is the Greatest?
Isaac O. Olaleye, 45

In the Shadow of a Rainbow
Robert Leslie Franklin, 72

In the Snow
Huy Voun Lee, 88

In the Year of the Boar and Jackie Robinson
Bette Bao Lord, 89

Inspirations: Stories of Women Artists
Leslie Sills, 165

Intrater, Roberta Grobel
Two Eyes, a Nose and a Mouth, 121

Invisible Hunters, The
Harriet Rohmer, 65

Invisible Princess, The
Faith Ringgold, 27

Ippisch, Hanneke
Sky: A True Story of Courage During World War II, 102

Ira Sleeps Over
Bernard Waber, 170

Irwin, Hadley
Kim/Kimi, 86
The Lilith Summer, 150

Isadora, Rachel
At the Crossroads, 41

It Doesn't Have to Be This Way: A Barrio Story/No Tiene Que Ser Asi: Una Historia Del Barrio
Luis Rodriguez, 65

It Takes a Village
Jane Cowen-Fletcher, 38

It's a Girl Thing: How to Stay Healthy, Safe, and In Charge
    Mavis Jukes, 163

J

Jackie Robinson and the Story of All-Black Baseball
    Jim O'Connor, 5

Jaffe, Nina
    The Golden Flower, 55

Jaguarundi
    Virginia Hamilton, 174

Jambo Means Hello
    Muriel Feelings, 40

Jar of Dreams
    Yoshiko Uchida, 94

Jaspersohn, William
    How the Forest Grew, 174

Jenness, Aylette
    Families: A Celebration of Diversity, Commitment and Love, 118

Jiminez, Francisco
    The Circuit: Stories from the Life of a Migrant Child, 55

Johnston, Tony
    The Wagon, 18

Join In: Multiethnic Short Stories by Outstanding Writers for Young Adults
    Donald Gallo, 107

Jojo's Flying Side Kick
    Brian Pinkney, 154

Jones, Adrienne
    Long Time Passing, 135

Jones, LeAlan, and Lloyd Newman
    Our America: Life and Death on the South Side of Chicago, 3

Jones, Jennifer Berry
    Heetunka's Harvest: A Tale of the Plains Indians, 75

Jordan, Sherryl
    The Raging Quiet, 144

Joseph, Lynn
    Coconut Kind of Day, 35

Journey for Peace: The Story of Rigoberta Menchu
    Marlene Targ Brill, 49

Journey Home
    Lawrence McKay, Jr., 89

Journey Home, The
    Yoshiko Uchida, 94

Journey, The: Japanese Americans, Racism and Renewal
    Sheila Hamanaka, 133

Journey of the Sparrows
    Fran Leper Buss with Daisy Cubias, 50

Journey to Jo'burg
    Beverly Naidoo, 44

Journey to Topaz
    Yoshiko Uchida, 94

Judge Rabbit and the Tree Spirit
    Lina Mao Wall, 95

Jukes, Mavis
    Growing Up: It's a Girl Thing, 163
    It's a Girl Thing: How to Stay Healthy, Safe and in Charge, 163

Julian's Glorious Summer
    Ann Cameron, 8

Julie of the Wolves
    Jean George, 72

Juniper
    Monica Furlong, 148

*Just Like Me: Stories and Self-
Portraits by 14 Artists*
  Harriet Rohmer, ed., 110

*Justin and the Best Biscuits
in the World*
  Mildred Pitts Walter, 170

K

Kamensky, Jane
  *Young Oxford History of Women
  in the United States. 2 The
  Colonial Mosaic: 1600-1760,* 167

Karhausen, Michael
  Children in China, 87

Kasza, Keiko
  A Mother for Choco, ix, 113

Kate Shelley and the Midnight Express
  Margaret Wetterer, 156

Katz, Karen
  The Colors of Us, 108
  Over the Moon, 114

Keenan, Sheila
  *Scholastic Encyclopedia of Women
  in the United States,* 164

*Keepers of the Animals: Native-
American Stories and Wildlife
Activities for Children*
  Joseph Bruchac and
  Michael J. Caduto, 179

*Keepers of the Earth:
Native-American Stories with
Environmental Activities for Children*
  Joseph Bruchac and
  Michael J. Caduto, 179

*Keepers of Life: Discovering Plants
Through Native-American Stories and
Earth Activities for Children*
  Joseph Bruchac and
  Michael J. Caduto, 179

*Keepers of the Night:
Native-American Stories and
Nocturnal Activities for Children*
  Joseph Bruchac and
  Michael J. Caduto, 179

Keister, Douglas
  *Fernando's Gift/
  El Regalo de Fernanco,* 175

Keller, Holly
  Grandfather's Dream, 87
  Horace, 114

Kerr, M. E.
  Night Kites, 129

Kheridian, David
  The Road from Home, 135

Kidd, Diana
  Onion Tears, 136

Kid's Guide to Social Action
  Barbara A.Lewis, 137

Kids Who Walk on Volcanoes
  Paul Otteson, 56

*Kids with Courage: True Stories About
Young People Making A Difference*
  Barbara A. Lewis, 136

Kim/Kimi
  Hadley Irwin, 86

Kindersley, Barnabas and Anabel
  Children Just Like Me, ix, 122
  *Children Just like Me:
  Celebrations,* 122

King, Martin Luther, Jr.
  I Have a Dream, 19

King's Equal, The
  Katherine Paterson, 153

Kingsolver, Barbara
  The Bean Trees, 150

Kiss the Dust
  Elizabeth Laird, 105

Kissinger, Katie
  All the Colors We Are/Todos los
  Colores de Nuestra Piel, ix, 108

Kivel, Paul
  Boys Will Be Men: Raising Our
  Sons for Courage, Caring and
  Commitment, 181

Knight, Margy Burns
  Talking Walls, 136
  Talking Walls:
  The Stories Continue, 136
  Welcoming Babies, 118
  Who Belongs Here?
  An American Story, 87

Kofi and His Magic
  Maya Angelou, 37

Kohn, Alfie
  The Schools Our Children Deserve:
  Moving Beyond Traditional
  Classrooms and "Tougher
  Standards," 181

Konecky, Edith
  Allegra Maud Goldman, 150

Kozol, Jonathan
  Savage Inequalities, 182

Krach, Maywan Shen
  D Is for Doufu: An Alphabet Book
  of Chinese Culture, 87

Kraft, Betsy Harvey
  Mother Jones: One Woman's Fight
  for Labor, 164

Kraus, Joanna Halpert
  Tall Boy's Journey, 114

Kreidler, William
  Creative Conflict Resolution: More
  Than 200 Activities for Keeping
  Peace in the Classroom, 182

Krementz, Jill
  How It Feels to Be Adopted, 115

Krescher, Joan
  My Mother's Getting Married, 118

Krull, Kathleen
  Wilma Unlimited, ix, 19

Kurdish Family
  Karen O'Connor, 108

Kurusa
  La Calle es Libre/
  The Streets Are Free, 62

Kusugak, Michael Avaarluk
  Hide and Sneak, 75
  A Promise Is a Promise, 75

Kwanzaa
  A.P. Porter, 25

Kwanzaa and Me: A Teacher's Story
  Vivian Paley, 185

L

Laird, Elizabeth
  Kiss the Dust, 105

Land of the Four Winds
  Veronica Freeman Ellis, 38

Lansky, Bruce, ed.
  Girls to the Rescue Series, 150

Lasky, Kathryn
  True North, 19
  She's Wearing a Dead Bird
  on Her Head, 151

Last Safe House, The: A Story of the
Underground Railroad
  Barbara Greenwood, 13

Last Summer with Maizon
  Jacqueline Woodson, 33

Lattimore, Deborah Nourse
  The Winged Cat, 105

Lauture, Denize
Running the Road to ABC, 35

Lawrence, Jacob
The Great Migration, 20

Leaf, Munro
El Cuento de Ferdinando, 62

Leder, Jane Nersky
Russian Jewish Family, 108

Lee, Enid, Deborah Menkhart and
Margaret Okazawa-Rey, ed.
Beyond Heroes and Holidays:
A Practical Guide to K-12
Antiracist, Multicultural Education
and Staff Development, 182

Lee, Huy Voun
At the Beach, 88
In the Park, 88
In the Snow, 88

Lee, Jeanne M.
Silent Lotus, 89
The Song of Mulan, 89

Lessac, Frane
My Little Island, 35

Lester, Julius
Long Journey Home, 4
This Strange New Feeling, 3
What a Truly Cool World, 20

Let the Circle Be Unbroken
Mildred Taylor, 30

Letters from Rifka
Karen Hesse, 101

Levine, David et al
Rethinking Schools: An Agenda
for Change, 183

Levine, Gail Carson
Dave at Night, 109

Levoy, Myron
Alan and Naomi, 102

Lewin, Ted
Market, 123

Lewis, Barbara A.
Kid's Guide to Social Action, 137
Kids with Courage: True Stories
About Young People Making a
Difference, 136
Lies My Teacher Told Me:
Everything Your American History
Book Got Wrong. 183
James W. Loewen, 183

Life Around the Lake: Embroideries by
the Women of Lake Patzcuaro
Maricel Presilla and
Gloria Soto, 57

Lights for Gita
Rachna Gilmore, 86

Like Sisters on the Homefront
Rita Williams-Garcia, 32

Lilith Summer, The
Hadley Irwin, 150

Lily Cupboard, The
Shulamith Levey Oppenheim,
102

Lindbergh, Reeve
Nobody Owns the Sky: The Story of
Brave Bessie Coleman, 151

Lindsay, Jeanne Warren
Do I Have a Daddy? A Story
About a Single-Parent Child, 118

Lion Dancer: Ernie Wan's Chinese
New Year
Kate Waters, 95

Listen to Us:
The World's Working Children
Jane Springer, 139

Little Weaver of Thai Yen Village
Tran-Khan Tuyet, 93

Littlechild, George
  This Land Is My Land, 76

Littlefield, Holly
  Fire at the Triangle Factory, 144

Littlesugar, Amy
  Tree of Hope, 20

*Lives Turned Upside Down:
Homeless Children in Their Own
Words and Photographs*
  Jim Hubbard, 144

Loewen, James W.
  *Lies My Teacher Told Me:
  Everything Your American History
  Book Got Wrong.* 183

London, Jonathan
  The Village Basket Weaver, 35

Long Journey Home
  Julius Lester, 4

Long Road, The
  Luis Garay, 53

Long Time Passing
  Adrienne Jones, 135

Lorax, The
  Dr. Seuss, 177

Lord, Betty Bao
  *In the Year of the Bear and
  Jackie Robinson,* 89

Lost Children, The
  Paul Goble, 74

Lotus Seed, The
  Sherry Garland, 85

*Love Makes a Family: Portraits of
Lesbian, Gay, Bisexual, and
Transgender Parents and Their
Families*
  Peggy Gillespie, 117

Loving
  Ann Morris
  and Ken Heyman, 123

Lowry, Linda
  Wilma Mankiller, 76

Lowry, Lois
  Number the Stars, 102

*Lucita Comes Home to Oaxaca/
Lucita Regresa a Oaxaca*
  Robin Cano, 60

Luenn, Nancy
  *A Gift for Abuelita: Celebrating the
  Day of the Dead,* 62
  Song for the Ancient Forest, 175

Lumpkin, Beatrice
  *Senefer: A Young Genius in
  Old Egypt,* 42

Lupita Manana
  Patricia Beatty, 49

Lyddie
  Katherine Paterson, 153

M

MacMillan, Bruce
  Mary Had a Little Lamb, 13

Macy, Sue
  *A Whole New Ball Game: The
  Story of the All-American Girls
  Professional Baseball League,* 164

*Magic Dogs of the Volcanoes/
Los Perros Magicos De Los Volcanes*
  Manlio Argueta, 59

Magid Fasts for Ramadan
  Mary Matthews, 105

Maid of the North
  Ethel Phelps, 157

Maizon at Blue Hill
  Jacqueline Woodson, 33

Make a Wish, Molly
  Barbara Cohen, 100

Malcolm X
  The Autobiography of Malcolm X,
  ix, 5

Malone, Michael
  Guatemalan Family, 108

Mama, Raouf
  *The Barefoot Book of
  Tropical Tales*, 123

Mandela
  Floyd Cooper, 38

Manitonquat
  *Children of the Morning Light:
  Wampanoag Tales*, 76

*Many Thousand Gone:
African Americans from Slavery to
Freedom*
  Virginia Hamilton, 14

Marcos, Subcomandante
  *The Story of the Colors/
  La Historia de los Colores*, 63

Margaret and Margarita
  Lynn Reiser, 64

Maria's Comet
  Deborah Hopkinson, 149

Mariscal, Blanca Lopez de
  *The Harvest Birds/
  Los Pajaros de la Cosecha*, 62

*Marisol and Magdalena: The Sound
of Our Sisterhood*
  Veronica Chambers, 51

Market
  Ted Lewin, 123

*Marriage of the Rain Goddess:
A South-African Myth*
  Olivia Wolfson, 47

Martinez, Alejandro Cruz
  *The Woman Who Outshone
  the Sun*, 63

Martinez, Victor
  Parrot in the Oven, 55

Mary Had a Little Lamb
  Sarah Josepha Hale, 13

Marx, Trish
  One Boy from Kosovo, 98

Marzollo, Jean
  *Happy Birthday,
  Martin Luther King*, 20

Mastoon, Adam
  *The Shared Heart:
  Portraits and Stories Celebrating
  Lesbian, Gay and Bisexual Young
  People*, ix, 129

Mathis, Sharon Bell
  Sidewalk Story, 21

Matthews, Mary
  Magid Fasts for Ramadan, 105

Maury, Inez
  My Mother the Mail Carrier, 63

May, Elaine Taylor
  *Young Oxford History of Women
  in the United States. 9 Pushing
  the Limits; 1940-1961*, 167

McCully, Emily Arnold
  Ballot Box Battle, 151
  The Bobbin Girl, 151
  Mirette on the High Wire, 152

McCurdy, Michael
  *Escape from Slavery:
  The Boyhood of Frederick
  Douglass in his Own Words*, 4

McCutcheon, John
  Happy Adoption Day!, 115

McDermott, Gerald
  Anansi the Spider, 42
  Flecha al Sol, 63

McDonough, Yona Zeldis
  *Sisters in Strength: American
  Women Who Made a Difference,*
  164

McGee, Charmayne
  So Sings the Deer, 76

McGill, Alice
  Molly Bannaky, ix, 152

McKee, Tim
  *No More Strangers Now: Young
  Voices from the New South Africa,*
  42

McKissack, Patricia
  The Dark-Thirty, 21
  Run Away Home, 21

Me and Alves: A Japanese Journey
  Terumasa Akio, 82

Me, Mop and the Moondance Kid
  Walter Dean Myers, 23

Mead, Alice
  Crossing the Starlight Bridge, 77

Medearis, Anglea Shelf
  *The Singing Man: Adapted from a
  West African Folktale,* 43
  Too Much Talk, 43

Mediopollito/ Half-Chicken
  Alma Flor Ada, 59

Meiko and the Fifth Treasure
  Eleanor Coerr, 132

Melzer, Milton
  *Black Americans: A History in
  Their Own Words,* 4

Mendez, Phil
  The Black Snowman, 22

Merriam, Eve
  The Wise Woman and Her Secret,
  153

Merrill, Yvonne
  *Hands on Asia: Art Activities for
  All Ages,* 184
  *Hands on Latin America:
  Art Activities for All Ages,* 183

*Mi Mama, La Cartera/
My Mother the Mail Carrier*
  Inez Maury, 63

Midwife's Apprentice, The
  Karen Cushman, 148

Miles, Miska
  Annie and the Old One, 77

Miller, William
  *Frederick Douglass: The Last Day
  of Slavery,* 4
  *Zora Hurston and the Chinaberry
  Tree,* 22

Milord, Susan
  *Tales of the Shimmering Sky:
  Ten Global Folktales with
  Activities,* 184

Minard, Rosemary
  Womenfolk and Fairy Tales, 158

*Minty: A Story of Young
Harriet Tubman*
  Alan Schroeder, 28

Miracle's Boys
  Jacqueline Woodson, 33

Mirette on the High Wire
  Emily Arnold McCully, 152

Mitchell, Margaree King
  Uncle Jed's Barbershop, 22

Mochizuki, Ken
  Baseball Saved Us, 137

Mohr, Nicholasa
  Felita, 55
  Going Home, 56

Moja Means One
  Muriel Feelings, 40

Mollel, Tololwa M.
  My Rows and Piles of Coins, 43
  Orphan Boy, 43
  Song Bird, 44

Molly Bannaky
  Alice McGill, ix, 152

Molly's Pilgrim
  Barbara Cohen, 101

Momaday, Natachee Scott
  Owl in the Cedar Tree, 77

Mommy Far, Mommy Near
  Carol Antoinette Peacock, 116

Monceaux, Morgan and
Ruth Katcher
  *Black and Red: Portraits of
  Independent Spirits*, 4

Mongolia
  Jan Reynolds, 125

Montejo, Victor
  *The Bird Who Cleans the World
  and Other Mayan Fables*, 56

Moody, Anne
  Coming of Age in Mississippi, 5

Moore, Yvette
  Freedom Songs, 22

Mora, Pat
  Pablo's Tree, 115

*More, More, More Said the Baby:
Three Love Stories*
  Vera B. Williams, 111

More Stories Julian Tells
  Ann Cameron, 8

Morning Girl
  Michael Dorris, 71

Morninghouse, Sundaira
  *Habari Gani? What's the News?
  A Kwanzaa Story*, 23

Moroney, Lynn
  *Elinda Who Danced in the Sky:
  An Estonian Folktale*, 98

Morris, Ann, and Ken Heyman
  Bread, Bread, Bread, 123
  Families, 123
  Hats, Hats, Hats, 123
  Houses and Homes, 123
  Loving, 123
  On the Go, 124
  Play, 124
  Shoes, Shoes, Shoes, 124
  Weddings, 124
  Work, 124

*Most Beautiful Place in the World,
The*
  Ann Cameron, 50

Mother for Choco, A
  Keiko Kasza, ix, 113

*Mother Jones: One Woman's Fight
for Labor*
  Betsy Harvey Kraft, 164

Mountains of Tibet, The
  Mordecai Gerstein, 85

Mrs. Katz and Tush
  Patricia Polacco, 110

Mufaro's Beautiful Daughters
  John Steptoe, 47

Mulberry Bird, The
  Anne Braff Brodzinsky, 112

*Multicultural Game Book, The:
More Than 70 Traditional Games
from 30 Countries, Grades 1-6*
  Louise Orlando, 184

Munsch, Robert
    The Paper Bag Princess, ix, 153
    *La Princesa Vestida con una Bolsa
    de Papel,* 64

Muse, Daphne, ed.
    Prejudice: A Story Collection, 109

Musgrove, Margaret
    Ashanti to Zulu, 44

My Dream of Martin Luther King, Jr.
    Faith Ringgold, 27

My Grandpa and the Sea
    Katherine Orr, 176

My Little Island
    Frané Lessac, 35

*My Mother the Mail Carrier/
Mi Mama, La Cartera*
    Inez Maury, 63

My Mother's Getting Married
    Joan Krescher, 118

My Rows and Piles of Coins
    Tololwa M. Mollel, 43

Myers, Walter Dean
    Brown Angels, 23
    Harlem, 23
    *Me, Mop and
    the Moondance Kid,* 23
    Won't Know Till I Get There, 24
    The Young Landlords, 24

N

Naidoo, Beverly
    Chain of Fire, 44
    Journey to J'burg, 44
    *No Turning Back:
    A Novel of South Africa,* 44

Namioka, Lensey
    April and the Dragon Lady, 90

*National Civil Rights Museum
Celebrates Everyday People, The*
    Alice Faye Duncan, 2

Native-American Animal Stories
    Joseph Bruchac, 69

Native-American Sign Language
    Madeline Olsen, 78

Native-American Stories
    Joseph Bruchac, 69

Native Dwelling Series
    Bonnie Shemie, 80

*Navajo: Visions and Voices
Across the Mesa*
    Shonto Begay, 66

Nelson, Pam
    *Cool Women: The Thinking Girl's
    Guide to the Hippest Women in
    the World,* 165

Nelson, S. D.
    Gift Horse, 77

Nettie's Trip South
    Ann Turner, 145

*New Kids in Town: Oral Histories of
Immigrant Teens*
    Jane Bode, 106

Newman, Leslea
    Heather Has Two Mommies, 129

Nez, Redwing T.
    Forbidden Talent, 78

Night Has Ears, The: African Proverbs
    Ashley Bryan, 38

Night Kites
    M.E. Kerr, 129

Night on Neighborhood Street
    Eloise Greenfield, 12

Nine O'Clock Lullaby
    Marilyn Singer, 125

Nine-in-One Grr! Grr!
  Blia Xiong, 95

Nino de Cabeza, El/
The Upside Down Boy
  Juan Felipe Herrera, 61

No Mirrors in My Nana's House
  Ysaye M.Barnwell, 7

No More Strangers Now: Young
Voices from the New South Africa
  Tim McKee, 42

No Tiene Que Ser Asi: Una Historia
de Barrio
  Luis Rodriguez, 65

No Turning Back:
A Novel of South Africa
  Beverly Naidoo, 44

Nobody Owns the Sky: The Story of
Brave Bessie Coleman
  Reeve Lindbergh, 151

Nodar, Carmen Santiago
  Abuelita's Paradise, 56

Not One Damsel in Distress:
World Folktales for Strong Girls
  Jane Yolen, 157

Number the Stars
  Lois Lowry, 102

Nye, Naomi Shihab
  Habibi, 137

O

O'Connor, Jim
  Jackie Robinson and the Story of
  All-Black Baseball, 5

O'Connor, Karen
  Kurdish Family, 108

Of Many Colors: Portraits of
Multi-racial Families
  Peggy Gillespie, 180

Ogbo:
Sharing Life in an African Village
  Ifeoma Onyefelu, 45

Oh, Kojo! How Could You!
  Verna Aardema, 37

Olaleye, Isaac O.
  In the Rainfield: Who Is
  the Greatest? 45

Oliver Button Is a Sissy
  Tomie DePaola, ix, 169

Olsen, Madeline
  Native-American Sign Language,
  78

On the Day You Were Born
  Debra Frasier, ix, 173

On the Go
  Ann Morris
  and Ken Heyman, 124

One Boy from Kosovo
  Trish Marx, 98

One Day We Had to Run!
Refugee Children Tell Their Stories in
Words and Paintings
  Sybella Wilkes in association
  with UNHCR
  and Save the Children, 47

One Grain of Rice:
A Mathematical Folktale
  Demi, 84

Onion Tears
  Diana Kidd, 136

Onyefelu, Ifeoma
  A Is for Africa 45
  Chidi Only Likes Blue: An African
  Book of Colors, 46
  Emeka's Gift: An African
  Counting Story, 46
  Ogbo: Sharing Life in an
  African Village, 45

Open Minds to Equality, 2nd Edition
Schniedewind, Nancy, and
Ellen Davidson, 186

Ophelia Speaks
Sarah Shandler, 165

Oppenheim, Shulamith Levey
The Lily Cupboard, 102

Orenstein, Peggy
Schoolgirls:
Young Women, Self Esteem and the
Confidence Gap, 184

Orgel, Doris
The Devil in Vienna, 103

Orie, Sandra De Coteau
Did You Hear the Wind Sing
Your Name?, 78

Orlando, Louise
The Multicultural Game Book:
More Than 70 Traditional Games
from 30 Countries, Grades 1-6, 184

Orphan Boy
Tololwa M. Mollel, 43

Orr, Katherine
My Grandpa and the Sea, 176
Story of a Dolphin, 175

Ortiz, Simon
The People Shall Continue, 78

Otteson, Paul
Kids Who walk on Volcanoes, 56

Our America: Life and Death on the
South Side of Chicago
LeAlan Jones
and Lloyd Newman, 3

Our Journey from Tibet
Laurie Dolphin, 84

Out From This Place
Joyce Hansen, 15

Out of the Dump: Writings and
Photographs by Children from
Guatemala
Kristen Franklin
and Nancy McGirr, 53

OutSpoken: Role Models from the
Lesbian and Gay Community
Michael Thomas Ford, 127

Over the Moon
Karen Katz, 114

Owl in the Cedar Tree
Natachee Scott Momaday, 77

P

Pablo Recuerda la Fiesta Del Dia
De Los Muertos
Jorge Ancona Diaz, 60

Pablo's Tree
Pat Mora, 115

Los Pajaros de la Cosecha/
The Harvest Birds
Blanca Lopez de Mariscal, 62

Paley, Vivian
Kwanzaa and Me:
A Teacher's Story, 185

Paper Bag Princess, The
Robert Munsch, ix, 153

Parks, Rosa
Dear Mrs. Parks: A Dialogue with
Today's Youth, 24
Rosa Parks: My Story, 24

Parrot in the Oven
Victor Martinez, 55

Pass It On: African-American Poetry
for Children
Wade Hudson, ed., 17

Paterson, Katherine
The King's Equal, 153
Lyddie, 153

Patterson, Eleanore
  Twice Upon a Time, 115

Peace Begins with You
  Katherine Scholes, 139

Peacock, Carol Antoinette
  Mommy Far, Mommy Near, 116

Peak, Min
  Aekyung's Dream, 90

Peineta Colorada, La/The Red Comb
  Fernando Pico, ix, 64

Pellegrini, Nina
  Families Are Different, 119

People Could Fly, The
  Virginia Hamilton, 14

People of the Breaking Day
  Marcia Sewall, 79

*People Power: A Look at Nonviolent
Action and Defense*
  Susan Nieburg Terkel, 139

People Shall Continue, The
  Simon Ortiz, 78

People Who Hugged the Trees
  Deborah Lee Rose, 91

*People's History of the United States,
Teaching Edition*
  Howard Zinn, ix, 187

Period
  JoAnn Gardner-Loulan, 162

*Perros Magicos, Los/
Magic Dogs of the Volcanos*
  Manlio Argueta, 59

Pettit, Jayne
  *A Time to Fight Back: True Stories
  of Wartime Resistance,* 138

Phelps, Ethel
  Maid of the North, 157
  Tatterhood and Other Tales, 158

Phoenix Rising
  Karen Hesse, 174

Picture Book of Anne Frank, A
  David Adler, 100

Pico, Fernando
  *La Peintata Colorado/
  The Red Comb,* ix, 64

Pink and Say
  Patricia Polacco, 138

Pinkney, Andrea Davis
  Alvin Ailey, 24
  Hold Fast to Dreams, 25
  Seven Candles for Kwanzaa, 25

Pinkney, Brian
  Jojo's Flying Side Kick, 154

Pipher, Mary
  *Reviving Ophelia; Saving the
  Selves of Adolescent Girls,* 185

Pirotta, Savior
  Turtle Bay, 90

Pitkanen, Matti
  Grandchildren of the Incas, 78

Play
  Ann Morris
  and Ken Heyman, 124

Polacco, Patricia
  Chicken Sunday, 109
  Mrs. Katz and Tush, 110
  Pink and Say, 138
  Tikvah Means Hope, 103
  Uncle Vova's Tree, 99

Pollack, William
  *Real Boys: Rescuing Our Sons
  from the Myths of Boyhood,* 185

Pomerantz, Charlotte
  The Princess and the Admiral, 154

Porter, A. P.
  Kwanzaa, 25

Prejudice: A Story Collection
  Daphne Muse, ed., 109

Presilla, Maricel and Gloria Soto
  *Life Around the Lake:
  Embroideries by the Women of
  Lake Patzcuaro,* 57

*Prietita and the Ghost Woman/
Prietita y La Llorona*
  Anzaldua, Gloria, 59

Prince Cinders
  Babette Cole, 168

*Princesa Vestida con una
Bolsa de Papel, La*
  Robert Munsch, 64

Princess and the Admiral, The
  Charlotte Pomerantz, 154

Princess Smartypants
  Babette Cole, 147

Promise Is a Promise, A
  Michael Avaarluk Kusugak and
  Robert Munsch, 75

Pueblo Storyteller
  Diane Hoyt-Goldsmith, 75

Q

*Quilted Landscape: Conversations
with Young Immigrants*
  Yale Strom, 110

R

Radio Man
  Arthur Dorros, 60

Ragan, Kathleen
  *Fearless Girls, Wise Women and
  Beloved Sisters: Heroines in
  Folktales from Around the World,*
  ix, 154

Raging Quiet, The
  Sherryl Jordan, 144

Rainbow People
  Laurence Yep, 97

Ramadan
  Suhaib Hamid Ghazi, 104

*Real Girl, Real World: Tools for
Finding Your True Self*
  Heather M Gray and
  Samantha Phillips, ix, 162

Real McCoy, The
  Wendy Towle, 31

Real, Elsa Okon
  *What Zeesie Saw on Delancey
  Street,* 103

*Real Boys: Rescuing Our Sons from the
Myths of Boyhood*
  William Pollack, 185

Real Sisters
  Susan Wright, 116

Red Comb, The/La Peintata Colorada
  Fernando Pico, ix, 64

Red Hawk, Richard
  *A, B, C's the American Indian
  Way,* 79

*Red Hawk's Account of Custer's
Last Battle*
  Paul Goble, 74

Reddix, Valerie
  Dragon Kite of the Autumn Moon,
  90

Reddy, Maureen
  *Everyday Acts Against Racism:
  Raising Children in a
  Multicultural Society,* 186

Reeder, Carolyn
  Shades of Gray, 138

Reflections of a Rock Lobster
  Aaron Fricke, 128

Reiser, Lynn
  Margaret and Margarita, 64

Remaking the Earth
  Paul Goble, 74

Remember Not to Forget
  Norman Finkelstein, 101

*Rethinking Schools:
An Agenda for Change*
  David Levine, et al, 183

Return of the Sun
  Joseph Bruchac, 69

*Reviving Ophelia: Saving the Selves of
Adolescent Girls*
  Mary Pipher, 185

Reynolds, Jan
  Amazon Basin, 124
  Down Under, 124
  Far North, 124
  Frozen North, 125
  Himalaya, 125
  Mongolia, 125
  Sahara, 125

*Ride on Mother's Back, A: A Day of
Baby Carrying Around the World*
  Emery and Durga Bernhard,
  120

Ringgold, Faith
  *Aunt Harriet's Underground
  Railroad in the Sky*, 26
  Bonjour, Lonnie, 26
  Counting to Tar Beach, 26
  Dinner at Aunt Connie's House, 26
  *If a Bus Could Talk: The Story of
  Rosa Parks*, 27
  The Invisible Princess, 27
  *My Dream of
  Martin Luther King, Jr.*, 27
  Tar Beach, 27

Rise Up Singing
  Peter Blood, 179

River Ran Wild, A
  Lynne Cherry, 173

Road from Home, The
  David Kherdian, 135

Road to Memphis, The
  Mildred Taylor, 31

Rodriguez, Luis
  *It Doesn't Have to Be This Way/
  No Tiene que ser Asi*, 65

Roe, Eileen
  *Con Mi Hermano/
  With My Brother*, 65

Rohmer, Harriet
  Atariba and Niguyona, 65
  The Invisible Hunters, 65
  *Just Like Me: Stories and
  Self-Portraits by 14 Artists*, 110
  Uncle Nacho's Hat, 65

Roll of Thunder, Hear My Cry
  Mildred Taylor, ix, 30

Romesburg, Dan
  *Young, Gay and Proud,
  4th Edition*, 130

Roop, Peter and Connie
  Ahyoka and the Talking Leaves,
  79

*Roots and Wings: Affirming Culture in
Early Childhood Settings*
  Stacey York, 187

Rosa Parks: My Story
  Rosa Parks, 24

Rose, Deborah Lee
  People Who Hugged the Trees, 91

Roses for Gita
  Rachna Gilmore, 85

Rostkowski, Margaret
  After the Dancing Days, 138

Run Away Home
  Patricia McKissack, 21

Running the Road to ABC
 Denize Lauture, 35

Russell, Ching Young
 First Apple, 91

Russian Jewish Family
 Jane Nersky Leder, 108

Ryder, Joanne
 Chipmunk Song, 176
 Snail's Spell, 176
 Where the Butterflies Grow, 176

S

Sachiko Means Happiness
 Kimiko Sakai, 91

Sacks, Margaret
 Beyond Safe Boundaries, 46

Sadako
 Eleanor Coerr, 132

*Sadako and the
Thousand Paper Cranes*
 Eleanor Coerr, 132

Sadker, Myra and David
 *Failing at Fairness: How Our
 Schools Cheat Girls*, 186

Sahara
 Jan Reynolds, 125

Sakai, Kimiko
 Sachiko Means Happiness, 91

Salmon, Marilyn
 *Young Oxford History of Women in
 the United States. 3 Limits of
 Independence: 1760-1800*, 167

Sami and the Time of the Troubles
 Florence Parry Heide and
 Judith Heide Gillil, 134

Sam's Passover
 Lynne Hannigan, 106

San Souci, Robert
 *Cut from the Same Cloth:
 American Women of Myth,
 Legend and Tall Tale*, 154
 The Faithful Friend, 36

Sanfield, Steve
 *Adventures of High John
 the Conqueror*, 28

Santiago, Chiori
 Home to Medicine Mountain, 79

Saturday Market, The
 Patricia Grossman, 53

Saturday Sancocho
 Leyla Torres, 57

Savage Inequalities
 Jonathan Kozol, 182

Save My Rainforest
 Monica Zak, 177

Shmidt, Jeremy
 Two Lands, One Heart, 91

Schniedewind, Nancy, and
Ellen Davidson
 *Open Minds to Equality,
 2nd Edition*, 186

*Scholastic Encyclopedia of the
North American Indian*
 James Ciment and
 Robert LaFrance, 70

*Scholastic Encyclopedia of Women in
the United States*
 Sheila Keenan, 164

Scholes, Katherine
 Peace Begins with You, 139

*Schoolgirls: Young Women,
Self Esteem and the Confidence Gap*
 Peggy Orenstein, 184

Schools Our Children Deserve, The: Moving Beyond Traditional Classrooms and "Tougher Standards"
Alfie Kohn, 181

Schroeder, Alan
Minty: A Story of Young Harriet Tubman, 28
The Stone Lion, 92

Schwartz, David M.
Supergrandpa, 99

Sciosca, Mary
Bicycle Rider, 28

Scooter
Vera B.Williams, 111

Seale, Doris
Through Indian Eyes: The Native Experience in Books for Children, 186

Secret of Gumbo Grove
Eleanora E. Tate, 29

Seigel, Beatrice
The Year They Walked, 5

Senefer: A Young Genius in Old Egypt
Beatrice Lumpkin, 42

Seth and Samona
Joanne Hyppolite, 18

Seuss, Dr.
The Lorax, 177

Seven Brave Women
Betsy Hearne, 149

Seven Candles for Kwanzaa
Andrea Davis Pinkney, 25

Sewall, Marcia
People of the Breaking Day, 79

Shabanu, Daughter of the Wind
Suzanne Fisher Staples ix, 155

Shades of Gray
Carolyn Reeder, 138

Shadows of the Night: The Hidden World of the Little Brown Bat
Barbara Bash, 172

Shandler, Sarah
Ophelia Speaks, 165

Shared Heart, The: Portraits and Stories Celebrating Lesbian, Gay and Bisexual Young People
Adam Mastoon, 129

Shea, Pegi Deitz
The Whispering Cloth, 92

Shemie, Bonnie
Native Dwelling Series

Houses of Bark: Tipi, Wigwam and Longhouse– The Woodland Indians, 80
Houses of Hide and Earth– The Plains Indians, 80
Houses of Snow, Skin and Bones– The Far North, 80
Houses of Wood– The Northwest Coast, 80

She's Wearing a Dead Bird on Her Head
Kathryn Lasky, 151

Shoes, Shoes, Shoes
Ann Morris
and Ken Heyman, 124

Sidewalk Story
Sharon Bell Mathis, 21

Sigerman, Harriet
Young Oxford History of Women in the United States. 5 Unfinished Battle: 1848-1865, 167
Young Oxford History of Women in the United States. 6 Laborers for Liberty: 1865-1890, 167
Young Oxford History of Women in the United States. 11 Biographical Supplement, 167

Silent Lotus
  Jeanne M. Lee, 89

Sills, Leslie
  *Inspirations: Stories of
  Women Artists,* 165
  *Visions: Stories of
  Women Artists,* 165

Sing, Rachel
  Chinese New Year's Dragon, 92

Singer, Bennett, ed.
  *Growing Up Gay:
  A Literary Anthology,* 130

Singer, Marilyn
  Nine O'Clock Lullaby, 125
  *Stay True: Short Stories for
  Strong Girls,* 155

*Singing Man, The: Adapted from a
West African Folktale*
  Angela Shelf Medearis, 43

Sirch, Willow Ann
  *Eco-Women: Protectors of the
  Earth,* 177

Sis, Peter
  Tibet Through the Red Box, 92

*Sisters in Strength: American Women
Who Made a Difference*
  Yona Zeldis McDonough, 164

Sisulu, Eleanor Batezat
  The Day Gogo Went to Vote, 46

Skutch, Robert
  Who's In a Family?, 119

*Sky: A True Story of Courage During
World War II*
  Hanneke Ippisch, 102

Smiling
  Gwenyth Swain, 126

Smith, Karen Manners
  *Young Oxford History of Women
  in the United States. 7 New Paths
  to Power: 1890-1920,* 167

Smith, Linda
  Dat's New Year, 106

Smoky Night
  Eve Bunting, 142

Smothers, Ethel Footman
  Down in the Piney Woods, 28

Snail's Spell
  Joanne Ryder, 176

So Far from the Sea
  Eve Bunting, 132

So Much
  Trish Cooke, 9

So Sings the Blue Deer
  Charmayne McGee, 76

Song Bird
  Tololwa M. Mollel, 44

Song for the Ancient Forest
  Nancy Luenn, 175

Song of Mulan, The
  Jeanne M. Lee, 89

Song of the Buffalo Boy
  Sherry Garland, 133

Song of the Trees
  Mildred Taylor, 30

Soto, Gary
  Too Many Tamales, 57

Soul Looks Back in Wonder
  Tom Feelings, ix, 11

*Sovietrek:
A Journey by Bicycle Across Russia*
  Dan Buettner, 98

*Spirit of the Maya: A Boy Explores
His People's Mysterious Past*
  Ted Wood, 58

Springer, Jane
    *Listen to Us: The World's
    Working Children*, 139

Stand Up for Your Rights
    World Book Encyclopedia, 140

Stanley, Jerry
    *I Am an American: The True Story
    of Japanese Internment*, 139

Staples, Suzanne Fisher
    Haveli, 155
    Shabanu, Daughter of the Wind,
    ix, 155

Star Fisher, The
    Laurence Yep, 97

Star Maiden, The
    Barbara Juster Esbensen, 71

*Stay True:
Short Stories for Strong Girls*
    Marilyn Singer, ed., 155

Steal Away
    Jennifer Armstrong, 6

Stellaluna
    Janell Cannon, 172

Steptoe, John
    Mufaro's Beautiful Daughters, 47

Stewart, Sarah
    The Gardener, 156

Stone, Susheila
    Eid-Ul-Fur, 107

Stone Lion, The
    Alan Schroeder, 92

Stories from the Silk Road
    Cherry Gilchrist, 85

Stories Huey Tells
    Ann Cameron, 9

Stories Julian Tells
    Ann Cameron, 8

Story of a Dolphin
    Katherine Orr, 175

*Story of the Colors, The/
La Historia de Los Colores*
    Subcomandante Marcos, 63

Story of the Milky Way, The
    Joseph Bruchac, 69

Streets Are Free, The/La Calle es Libre
    Kurusa, 62

Strickland, Dorothy
and Michael, illus.
    *Families: Poems Celebrating the
    African-American Experience*, 28

Strike
    Maureen Bayless, 131

Strom, Yale
    *Quilted Landscape: Conversations
    with Young Immigrants*, 110

Stroud, Bettye
    Down Home at Miss Dessa's, 29

Supergrandpa
    David M. Schwartz, 99

Surat, Michele
    Angel Child, Dragon Child, 93

Sutton, Roger
    *Hearing Us Out: Voices from the
    Lesbian and Gay Community*, 130

Swain, Gwenyth
    Carrying, 126
    Celebrating, 126
    Eating, 126
    Smiling, 126

Swamp, Chief Jake
    *Giving Thanks: A Native-
    American American Good
    Morning Message*, 80

Sweet Clara and the Freedom Quilt
    Deborah Hopkinson, 17

*Sweet Dried Apples: A Vietnamese
Wartime Childhood*
Rosemary Breckler, 131

Sweet Whispers, Brother Rush
Virginia Hamilton, 14

*Sweet Words So Brave: The Story of
African-American Literature*
Barbara Curry and
James Michael Brody, 10

T

*Tales of the Shimmering Sky:
Ten Global Folktales with Activities*
Susan Milord, 184

Talking Earth
Jean George, 72

Talking Walls
Margy Burns Knight, 136

Talking Walls: The Stories Continue
Margy Burns Knight, 136

Tall Boy's Journey
Joanna Halpert Kraus, 114

Tap-Tap
Karen Lynn Williams, 36

Tar Beach
Faith Ringgold, 27

Tarpley, Natasha Anastasia
I Love My Hair!, 29

Taste of Salt, A
Francis Temple, 36

Tate, Eleanora E.
*Front Porch Stories
at the One-Room School, 29
Secret of Gumbo Grove, 29
Thank You,
Dr. Martin Luther King, 29*

Tatterhood and Other Tales
Ethel Phelps, 158

Tatum, Beverly Daniels
*Why Are All the Black Kids Sitting
Together in the Cafeteria?, 187*

Tax, Meredith
Families, 119

Taylor, Mildred
*Let the Circle Be Unbroken, 30
The Road to Memphis, 31
Roll of Thunder, Hear My Cry,
ix, 30
Song of the Trees, 30
The Well, 31*

*Teaching for Diversity and
Social Justice: A Sourcebook*
Maurianne Adams,
Lee Anne Bell, Pat Griffin, 178

*Teaching for Social Justice:
A Democracy and Education Reader*
William Ayers, Jean Ann Hunt,
Therese Quinn, 178

*Teenage Guy's Survival Guide, The:
The Real Deal on Girls, Growing Up
and Other Guy Stuff*
Jeremy Daldry, 169

*Tell Me Again About
the Night I Was Born*
Jamie Lee Curtis, 113

Tell No One Who You Are
Walter Burchignani, 100

*Tell Them We Remember:
The Story of the Holocaust*
Susan D. Bacharach, 100

Temple, Francis
*Grab Hands and Run, 57
A Taste of Salt, 36*

Terkel, Susan Nieburg
*People Power: A Look at
Nonviolent Action and Defense,
139*

Thank You, Dr. Martin Luther King
  Eleanora E. Tate, 29

Thank You, Jackie Robinson
  Barbara Cohen, 101

Thimmesh, Catherine
  *Girls Think of Everything: Stories
  of Inventions by Women,* 166

Thirteen Moons on a Turtle's Back
  Joseph Bruchac,
  with Joseph London, 69

Thirty-Three Multicultural Tales to Tell
  Pleasant DeSpain, 180

This Land Is My Land
  George Littlechild, 76

This Land Is Your Land
  Woody Guthrie, paintings by
  Kathy Jakobsen, 133

This Strange New Feeling
  Julius Lester, 3

*Three Little Wolves and the
Big Bad Pig, The*
  Eugene Trivizas, 140

*Through Indian Eyes: The Native
Experience in Books for Children*
  Doris Seale, 186

*Through Moon and Stars
and Night Skies*
  Ann Turner, 116

Through My Eyes
  Ruby Bridges, 1

*Thunder Bear and Ko: The Buffalo
Nation and Nambe Pueblo*
  Susan Hazen-Hammond, 74

Tibet Through the Red Box
  Peter Sis, 92

Tikvah Means Hope
  Patricia Polacco, 103

Time of Angels, A
  Karen Hesse, 134

*Time to Fight Back, A: True Stories of
Wartime Resistance*
  Jayne Pettit, 138

To Be a Drum
  Evelyn Coleman, 9

Toestomper and the Caterpillars
  Sharleen Collicott, 168

Tomàs and the Library Lady
  Raul Colon, 51

Tomlinson, Theresa
  The Forest Wife, 156

Tonight Is Carnival
  Arthur Dorros, 52

Too Many Tamales
  Gary Soto, 57

Too Much Talk
  Angela Shelf Medearis, 43

Torres, Leyla
  Saturday Sancocho, 57

Trail of Tears, The
  Joseph Bruchac, 70

Tree of Hope
  Amy Littlesugar, 20

*Tree of Life:
The World of the African Baobab*
  Barbara Bash, 172

Trivizas, Eugene
  *The Three Little Wolves and the
  Big Bad Pig,* 140

Trottier, Maxine
  The Walking Stick, 93

True North
  Kathryn Lasky, 19

Turner, Ann
  Nettie's Trip South, 145
  Through Moon and Stars and Night Skies, 116

Turner, Glenette Tilley
  Follow in Their Footsteps: Biographies of Ten Outstanding African Americans, 5

Turner, Robin Montana
  Georgia O'Keefe, 166

Tuyet, Tran-Khan
  Little Weaver of Thai Yen Village, 93

Twice Upon a Time
  Eleanore Patterson, 115

Two Eyes, a Nose and a Mouth
  Roberta Grobel Intrater, 121

Two Lands, One Heart
  Jeremy Schmidt, 91

Two Teenagers in Twenty: Writing by Gay and Lesbian Youth
  Ann Heron, 128

U

Uchida, Yoshiko
  The Best Bad Thing, 94
  The Bracelet, 140
  Jar of Dreams, 94
  The Journey Home, 94
  Journey to Topaz, 94

Uncle Jed's Barbershop
  Margaree King Mitchell, 22

Uncle Nacho's Hat
  Harriet Rohmer, 65

Uncle Vova's Tree
  Patricia Polacco, 99

Uncle Willie and the Soup Kitchen
  Dyanne DiSalvo-Ryan, 143

Under the Lemon Moon
  Edith Hope Fine, ix, 52

Underground Railroad, The
  Raymond Bial, 1

Up in the Air: The Story of Bessie Coleman
  Philip Hart, 162

Upside Down Boy, The/ El Nino de Cabeza
  Juan Felipe Herrera, 61

Us and Them: A History of Intolerance in America
  Jim Carnes, 142

V

Very Last First Time, The
  Jan Andrews, 66

Viesti, Joe, and Diane Hall
  Celebrate! In Southeast Asia, 94
  Celebrate! In South Asia, 94

Village Basket Weaver, The
  Jonathan London, 35

Visions: Stories of Women Artists
  Leslie Sills, 165

Voices from the Streets; Former Gang Members Tell Their Stories
  S. Beth Atkin, 141

Voices of a Generation: Teenage Girls Report About Their Lives Today
  Pamela Haag, 181

W

Waber, Bernard
  Ira Sleeps Over, 170

Wagon, The
  Tony Johnston, 18

Wagon Wheels
  Barbara Brenner, 7

Waiting for the Rain
Sheila Gordon, 41

Wake Up, World: A Day in the Life of Children around the World
Beatrice Hollyer, 121

Walking Stick, The
Maxine Trottier, 93

Wall, Lina Mao
Judge Rabbit and the Tree Spirit, 95

Walter, Mildred Pitts
Justin and the Best Biscuits in the World, 170

Waters, Kate
Lion Dancer: Ernie Wan's Chinese New Year, 95

Watsons Go to Birmingham-1963, The
Christopher Paul Curtis, ix, 10

Way Out of No Way, A
Jacqueline Woodson, ed., 34

We Adopted You, Benjamin Koo
Linda Walvoord Girard, 113

Weddings
Ann Morris
and Ken Heyman, 124

Weed Is a Flower, A
Aliki, 1

Weighing the Elephant
Ting-xing Ye, 95

Welcome to the Green House
Jane Yolen, 177

Welcoming Babies
Margy Burns Knight, 118

Well, The
Mildred Taylor, 31

Wells, Rosemary
Yoko, 110

Wesley, Valerie
Freedom's Gifts: A Juneteenth Story, 32

Wetterer, Margaret
Kate Shelley and the Midnight Express, 156

What a Truly Cool World
Julius Lester, 20

What Are You? Voices of Mixed-Race Young People
Pearl Fuyo Gaskins, 107

What Zeesie Saw on Delancey Street
Elsa Okon Real, 103

When Birds Could Talk and Bats Could Sing
Virginia Hamilton, 13

When Clay Sings
Byrd Baylor, 66

Where Fireflies Dance/ Ahi, Donde Bailan los Luciernagas
Lucha Corpi, 60

Where the Butterflies Grow
Joanne Ryder, 176

Which Way Freedom?
Joyce Hansen, 15

Whispering Cloth
Pegi Deitz Shea, 92

White Socks Only
Evelyn Coleman, 9

Who Belongs Here? An American Story
Margy Burns Knight, 87

Whole New Ball Game, A: The Story of the All-American Girls Professional Baseball League
Sue Macy, 164

Who's Calling the Shots?
How to Respond Effectively to
Kids' Fascination with War Play
and War Toys
  Nancy Carlsson-Paige and
  Diane Levin, 180

Who's in a Family?
  Robert Skutch, 119

Who's in Rabbit's House?
  Verna Aardema, 37

Why Are All the Black Kids Sitting
Together in the Cafeteria?
  Beverly Daniels Tatum, 187

Why Did It Happen? Helping
Children Cope in a Violent World
  Janice Cohn, 143

Why Rat Comes First
  Clara Yen, 96

Wilkes, Sybella
  One Day We Had to Run!
  Refugee Children Tell Their Stories
  in Words and Pictures, 47

Willhoite, Michael
  Daddy's Roommate, 130

Williams, Arlene
  Dragon Soup, 157

Williams, Karen Lynn
  Galimoto, 47
  Tap-Tap, 36

Williams, Sherley Anne
  Working Cotton, 32

Williams, Vera B.
  More, More, More Said the Baby:
  Three Love Stories, 111
  Scooter, 111

Williams-Garcia, Rita
  Like Sisters on the Homefront, 32

Wilma Mankiller
  Linda Lowry, 76

Wilma Unlimited
  Kathleen Krull, ix, 19

Winged Cat, The
  Deborah Nourse Lattimore, 105

Wise Child
  Monica Furlong, 148

Wise Woman and Her Secret
  Eve Merriam, 153

With My Brother/Con Mi Hermano
  Eileen Roe, 65

Wolf, Bernard
  Cuba: After the Revolution, 58
  Homeless, 145

Wolfson, Evelyn
  From Abenaki to Zuni:
  A Dictionary of Native-American
  Tribes, 81

Wolfson, Olivia
  Marriage of the Rain Goddess:
  A South-African Myth, 47

Woman Who Outshone the Sun, The
  Alejandro Cruz Martinez, 63

Women of Hope: African Americans
Who Made a Difference
  Joyce Hansen, 162

Womenfolk and Fairy Tales
  Rosemary Minard, 158

Wonderful Towers of Watts, The
  Patricia Zelver, 111

Won't Know Till I Get There
  Walter Dean Myers, 24

Wood, Ted
  A Boy Becomes a Man at
  Wounded Knee, 81
  Spirit of the Maya: A Boy Explores
  His People's Mysterious Past, 58

Woodson, Jacqueline
    *Between Madison and
    Palmetto, 33*
    The Dear One, 34
    *From the Notebooks of
    Melanin Sun, 33*
    Last Summer with Maizon, 33
    Maizon at Blue Hill, 33
    Miracles' Boys, 33
    A Way Out of No Way, 34

Work
    Ann Morris,
    and Ken Heyman, 124

Working Cotton
    Sherley Anne Williams, 32

World Book Encyclopedia
    Stand Up for Your Rights, 140

Wright, Susan
    Real Sisters, 116

✗

Xiong, Blia
    Nine-in-One Grr! Grr!, 95

Xuan, Yong-Sheng
    *The Dragon Lover and Other
    Chinese Proverbs, 95*

Y

Yarbrough, Camille
    Cornrows, 34

Ye, Ting-xing
    Weighing the Elephant, 95

Year They Walked, The
    Beatrice Seigel, 5

Yen, Clara
    Why Rat Comes First, 96

Yep, Laurence
    The Amah, 96
    Child of the Owl, 96
    Dragonwings, ix, 97
    Rainbow People, 97
    The Star Fisher, 97

Yoko
    Rosemary Wells, 110

Yolen, Jane
    The Devil's Arithmetic, 103
    *Not One Damsel in Distress: World
    Folktales for Strong Girls, 157*
    Welcome to the Green House, 177

York, Stacey
    *Roots and Wings:
    Affirming Culture in Early
    Childhood Settings, 187*

Young, Gay and Proud, 4th Edition
    Dan Romesburg, 130

Young Landlords, The
    Walter Dean Myers, 24

*Young Oxford History of Women
in the United States. 1 The Tried and
The True: Native-American Women
Confronting Colonization*
    John Demos, 166

*Young Oxford History of Women
in the United States. 2 The Colonial
Mosaic: 1600-1760*
    Jane Kamensky, 167

*Young Oxford History of Women in
the United States. 3 Limits of
Independence.: 1760-1800*
    Marilyn Salmon, 167

*Young Oxford History of Women in
the United States. 4 Breaking New
Ground: 1800-1848*
    Michael Goldberg, 167

Young Oxford History of Women in the United States. 5 Unfinished Battle: 1848-1865
  Harriet Sigerman, 167

Young Oxford History of Women in the United States. 6 Laborers for Liberty: 1865- 1890
  OHarriet Sigerman, 167

Young Oxford History of Women in the United States. 7 New Paths to Power: 1890-1920
  Karen Manners Smith, 167

Young Oxford History of Women in the United States. 8 From Ballots to Breadlines: 1920-1940
  Sarah Jane Deutsch, 167

Young Oxford History of Women in the United States. 9 Pushing the Limits: 1940-1961
  Elaine Taylor May, 167

Young Oxford History of Women in the United States. 10 The Road to Equality: 1962-present
  William H.Chafe, 167

Young Oxford History of Women in the United States. 11 Biographical Supplement
  Harriet Sigerman, 167

Z

Zachary's New Home: A Story for Foster and Adopted Children
  Geraldine Blomquist, 112

Zak, Monica
  Save My Rainforest, 177

Zamani Goes to Market
  Muriel Feelings, 40

Zelver, Patricia
  The Wonderful Towers of Watts, 111

Zinn, Howard
  People's History of the United States, Teaching Edition, ix, 187

Zipes, Jack
  Don't Bet on the Prince, 158

Zora Hurston and the Chinaberry Tree
  William Miller, 22